EARTH

my life is ful field.

Peter

Foreword by NASA Astronaut Jack Lousma

Earth Angels

The Story of
Peter VandenBosch *and*
Wings of Mercy

as told to

Milton Nieuwsma

EARTH ANGELS
The Story of Peter VandenBosch and Wings of Mercy
© 2011 Milton Nieuwsma

Author's Note: This is my story; the events recalled in this book are true to the best of my memory. All the people portrayed in this book are, or were, actual living persons. However, some names have been changed to protect their privacy.

Published by
Deep River Books
Sisters, Oregon
http://www.deepriverbooks.com

ISBN 13 978-1-935265-96-2
ISBN-10 1-935265-96-2

Library of Congress: 2011935712

Printed in the USA

To Joan,
the love of my life,
who encouraged me to spread my wings
and earned hers in the process

The Legend of the Green Stick

Leo Tolstoy, the great Russian writer, believed a green stick was buried near his home that carried the secret of everlasting happiness. He spent most of his life in a quest for the Green Stick. This is the story of my quest for the Green Stick and how I found it.

PVB

CONTENTS

ACKNOWLEDGMENTS

THANK YOU, JAY PETERS, for encouraging me to write this book. Special thanks to Milton Nieuwsma for helping me accomplish this task. His insight into my life and heart and understanding of sensitive situations revealed his unusual talent as a writer and editor. Greg Nieuwsma, Milt's son, researched and wrote much of the material and interviewed the patients and families featured in this book.

Thanks to Jack Lousma, the former NASA astronaut and one of Wings of Mercy's earliest proponents, for writing the foreword. Among his many contributions to America's space program, he is probably best remembered as the ground control recipient of the "Houston, we've got a problem" call from Apollo 13.

Bill Stehouwer, my father-in-law, supported and encouraged me in my vision for Wings of Mercy from its inception. It was he who said, "By what right do you think you must keep this organization here in Western Michigan?" Dad is gone now, but he will always have an honored place in Wings of Mercy's history.

Thanks to Jim and Ginger Jurries, Rick and Jill Siegers, Bob and Anne Geurink, and Joan VandenBosch, in honor of her father, Bill Stehouwer, for their financial support of this project. Because of them, all of the sales proceeds from this book will go to Wings of Mercy, Inc.

Carleton Wright, Jr., a former FAA examiner, established the technical bylaws and wrote the first pilot guidelines for Wings of Mercy. Jay Van-Daalen, the first pilot/aircraft owner to join Wings of Mercy, helped me through the organizational phase. Thank you, Carl and Jay.

Thanks to Sharon Huminsky, Grace Spelde and my wife Joan. They deserve my appreciation for the help they gave in so many ways, from coordinating interviews for this book to providing details from the Wings of Mercy office, and the book cover design.

Finally, my thanks go to the three hundred volunteer pilots who have flown Wings of Mercy missions since the organization began in 1991. In my book each one deserves the title, "Earth Angel."

—PETER J. VANDENBOSCH

FOREWORD
BY COL. JACK R. LOUSMA (USMC, RET.)

TWO GENERATIONS AGO, PETER VANDENBOSCH grew up in a large farm family near Edgerton, Minnesota, where he learned the virtues of integrity, hard work, self-discipline, and a host of other principles and values embedded in America's earliest foundations. He was among the many of that generation who were driven by faithfulness to God, patriotism to America, and responsibility to family. In his formative years, secularism was not interfering with his religious beliefs, most of our citizens sacrificed along with our troops in wartime, and personal responsibility trumped government interference in our lives.

The message of *Earth Angels* is that Peter has lived a most rewarding, God-honoring life of purpose, meaning and fulfillment for over four-score years without wavering from his youthful underpinnings. He did this despite temptations to do it "my way" and the intervening decline of the fundamental foundations and traditions upon which America was originally established. Hopefully, Peter's story will inspire our generation to document and pass on to succeeding generations the conservative principles and values that have embodied the "Greatest Generation."

I believe that Pete, as his friends call him, when he left the farm after high-school with only a few dollars in his pocket, had little idea of where life would take him except that he enjoyed music and wanted to fly airplanes. In those days aviation was a very risky profession but one with excitement and adventure written all over it. I also surmise Pete left the farm believing strongly that living a godly life would yield favorable outcomes. In fact, about that time, his mother had prayed with him and asked God to "guide Peter to make the decision that will please you in his life."

Besides the guidance we receive from the Bible, God often uses other people, our conscience, or life's circumstances to get His message across to us. I presume Peter made that decision about which his mother prayed, to become a follower of Jesus Christ. So, he left home with a "right relationship" with God and a sense that, with an obedient spirit, God would direct his future.

Pete found some odd jobs to support himself independently after leaving the farm. After all, his father told him as he departed that he had chosen to depart and not to expect to return for a handout. Such a reminder was not meant to be derogatory; rather, it was a long-standing custom in the Dutch immigrant community. Pete's passion for aviation and his future employment were both accommodated when World War II began with the bombing of Pearl Harbor in 1941. In those days, any healthy man of war-fighting age either joined the military service or was often shunned as a shirker of duty, since all able-bodied males across the nation either volunteered or would be drafted into the military service unless a family hardship or disqualifying medical reason could be demonstrated. Pete, then only 18 years old, viewed enlistment as both a patriotic responsibility and an answer to prayer because now he could pursue his fascination with aviation by enlisting in the Army Air Corps while also getting a paycheck, his board and room paid, and a clearly-defined direction for his life until the war was over.

After enlisting, Pete's entry into aviation was nearly terminated due to an inexplicable medical problem. This prospect was devastating to him, but he recalled a minister had told him while grieving after a family tragedy on the farm that "God had a plan for everyone." God again sent him a message, this time through the hospital chaplain who discovered Pete's ambition to fly was shared by his passion for music. The chaplain told him, "I think God has a plan for you!" Pete was asked to organize a military choir and to direct a concert for the troops, as well as to sing tenor regularly with a men's octet on Armed Forces Radio! After this prophetic interlude, Pete's medical anomaly was resolved, and he was assigned to a crew flying combat missions in B-24 Liberator bombers over Europe until the war in that theater ended in 1945. Pete was still only 22 years old, but his experiences had matured him beyond his years.

Peter's early upbringing and his military experiences were God's way of enabling him to develop the interests, skills, and talent that would shape the rest of his life and professional career and even throughout his retirement years. They also imbued him with the faith, leadership, and audacity it takes to assume risks, pioneer new enterprises, and to draw out the best in other people. He applied his God-given gifts in music to originate and, for many years, direct two sacred music groups; the King's Choraliers and the Metropolitan Choir of Praise. Meanwhile, he was also building and expanding a business in radio broadcasting. He ultimately acquired Midwest radio stations, as well as a private pilot's license and an airplane to commute between them. By the time he was comfortably retired, God had blended Peter's compassionate heart and pioneering spirit with the leadership, management, and flying skills necessary to rouse him back into action to establish, although he did not know it yet, the Wings of Mercy.

One day, after Peter and his discerning wife, Joan, had become comfortable in a well-deserved retirement for several years, Peter was enjoying the magnificence of the 'Good Earth' in near solitude when God captured his attention in a most unusual and unmistakable way. This time it was not through another person, his conscience, or a circumstance, as it had been previously. I sincerely believe it happened exactly as Peter describes it. It was so unusual for the era in which we are living that Pete knew God meant business. What God wanted to convey was articulated so powerfully that it could be neither doubted nor declined; no turning back! Pete did not know what this new mission was, but he had the faith and trust to know the same God who interrupted his reverie would direct him according to His purpose. Ultimately, and with Joan's added sensitivity to God's call, Peter organized and led the Wings of Mercy, beginning in 1991.

All of this simply demonstrates that God does have a plan for committed believers like Peter, or like you and me. Further, His plan is always better than one we could ever lay out for ourselves. He is never finished with us, and He never makes mistakes!

Over the past 20 years, Wings of Mercy has flown over 5,500 missions transporting low-income adults and children with illnesses, diseases, and handicaps that cannot be treated locally to specialty medical centers in the United States and Canada to which they cannot afford to travel. Hundreds of highly experienced and certified pilots have volunteered their time and skills to fly these patients in dozens of well-maintained airplanes donated by their owners for these missions of mercy. The flight operations and patient comfort of Wings of Mercy are professional and caring to a fault.

Contributors are assured that nearly 100 percent of their donations to Wings of Mercy go directly to accomplishing its mission. The lives improved and saved by Wings of Mercy flights are beyond counting, and the gratitude of patients is expressed emotionally and profusely. All who are involved in accomplishing the missions realize a rewarding sense of purpose and fulfillment. They are personally grateful for the privilege of serving and caring in a manner that far outweighs the time and effort offered, once again affirming what Jesus said, "It is more blessed to give than to receive."

—JACK R. LOUSMA COLONEL, USMC (RET.)
FORMER NASA ASTRONAUT

Jack Lousma was one of nineteen NASA astronauts selected for the Apollo space program in 1966. He served on the support crew for Apollo 9, 10 and 13 and piloted Skylab-3. In 1975 he served as the backup docking module pilot for the historic U.S./Soviet Apollo-Soyuz Test Project and later commanded the third Columbia space shuttle mission. In 1982 he was inducted into the International Space Hall of Fame.

PART ONE

The Green Stick

Chapter One

'Honey, there's something
I have to tell you'

Some people just have a knack. Like the guy Alistair Cooke talked about in an episode of his popular 1970s television series, *America*. The episode, called "Money on the Land," described how the late 19th century financial barons like the Rockefellers and Carnegies and Vanderbilts acquired their fortunes. Filming in Andrew Carnegie's personal library, a treasure-trove of priceless first editions at his Newport mansion, Mr. Cooke peered into the camera and asked, "What did these people have that the rest of us don't have?" It had nothing to do with general intelligence, he said. What they had was a knack, an aptitude for fortune-making, as one might have a knack for cabinet-making. He then told about a man who spoke sixteen languages, all fluently, but couldn't say anything sensible in any of them.

Joe Mutter had a knack. It wasn't a knack for making money or learning foreign languages, although he spoke a little German. His knack was fishing for grouper. Nobody knew how to do it like Joe. If there ever was an old salt, it was Joe. He was gruff and irritable and short in stature and social graces. But he knew how to fish, and he knew how to find grouper in the Gulf of Mexico.

I always suspected that Joe, a retired German sea captain, had been on the other side in the war, but I never brought it up. After all, my fishing buddies Al and Indie and I were veterans from the American side, and what was past was past. We had long buried our bombs and hand grenades, and we were using radar to track fish, not the enemy.

Joe knew just how to do it. He'd say, "Forget your latitude and longitude markings. We're starting from scratch." Then out we'd go, from Wiggins Pass into the Gulf.

Our fishing boat was a 25-foot Tiara, the finest money could buy, with a center console and two 150-horsepower engines. Man, she was a beauty. As we headed out to sea, the land would sink out of sight at seven or eight miles, the trees at ten miles, the high rises along the Naples shoreline at eleven or twelve. Then we'd go for another hour and stop. Not a tree or building in sight, nothing, except for a cruise ship now and then on the horizon or another fishing boat that I suspected might be following us, because Joe had quite a reputation as a fish-finder.

Finally he'd cut the engines and shout, "Drop the anchor!" Usually it was Al Zimmerman up in the bow who threw out the anchor. Then Joe would instruct us to start counting, "One…two…three…," and the boat would begin to drift. At the count of six Indie and I would drop a floater on each side of the boat, so when the wind shifted we'd know exactly how far off the point we were, the point where Joe had spotted a school of grouper eighty feet down hugging the bottom of the sea. He just had that knack.

Joe always knew where the fish were, and always we'd come back with a huge catch. The other fishermen back at the marina would be astounded. "Where did you catch all those fish?" they'd ask.

Even the Bonita Springs newspaper got wind of our good fortune. One day a photographer showed up at our marina and took pictures of me and my buddies with our catch of the day—enough to feed eighty of our neighbors.

※〜 ※〜 ※〜

November is the best time of the year to fish in the Gulf. The hurricanes are mostly gone, and the days are invariably sunny but hot and humid. It was on just such a day in November 1990, two weeks before Thanksgiving, that we maneuvered our way out through Wiggins Pass into the Gulf. The sun was still at our backs when we hit open water.

Two hours later, Joe ordered Al to drop anchor. Indie and I followed with the floaters and the counting. We assumed our usual places along the rail: Al and Indie in the bow, Joe on starboard, I on portside. Thirty-five miles out, the water was as smooth as glass.

As I gazed out from the rail, it struck me that I was doing exactly what so many men dream of doing when they retire. When it came my turn in 1984, I had accomplished most of the things I had set out to do. I had owned two radio stations back in Michigan. I had founded two choral groups and staged over five hundred concerts. I had even recorded several albums. I was blissfully married to my second wife, Joan.

These were the things I would ponder as I gazed out on the water, waiting for a grouper to pull my line. None of us in the boat spoke at times like this. We had but one purpose: to catch groupers, to catch as many as we could. Our mission was singular and uncomplicated, and the results were easy to measure. We could catch as many grouper as we wanted. Perhaps we would set a new record this time. Perhaps we would catch enough grouper to feed a *hundred* people. These were the thoughts that ran through my head as I sat there on the deck on this glorious November day, thirty-five miles out from the Florida shore. Yes, life was good.

Then I heard a voice. "Peter," it said.

I turned around and looked at Al and Indie and Joe. All three were gazing out over the water; it was obvious none of them had said anything. I turned back and checked my line.

"Peter."

I looked at my buddies again. Nothing, no sign that any of them had said—or heard—anything.

"Peter," the voice said again. This time it was more distinct—soft and gentle yet more distinct. "Peter," it said, "there is more to life than this."

I looked at Al and Indie and Joe. Again, nothing.

Once more the voice spoke. This time it was more like an echo: *"Peter, there is more to life than this."*

I tried to busy myself. Reaching out to check the bait on my line, my hand quivered. I felt blood rushing from my head down to my feet. "I mustn't faint," I told myself. "I mustn't say a word. What if my buddies notice?"

I tried to steady one hand with the other as I pulled in the line, but my heart was racing. Was it racing to pump blood back up to my head? Was I still going to faint? Please, God, don't let me faint, or Joe won't take me fishing again. He'll think I'm a wimp. Surely Al and Indie will think so too.

Finally we pulled in our lines. It was 2:30 in the afternoon and a two-and-a-half-hour journey back.

By the time we reached Wiggins Pass the sun was at our backs. I hadn't said a word to my buddies the whole time. All the while the thought kept running through my head: Was the voice real? Did I really hear it? Whose voice was it?

I don't remember scrubbing the boat or saying good-bye to my buddies after we fished that day. I do remember driving home—we lived two miles from the marina at a resort called Lake San Marino—and I remember taking a shower, because Joan always complained I smelled like fish when I got home. After we finished dinner, I got up from the table and said, "I'm going for a walk."

"Don't you want me to go with you?" she asked.

"No, I need to go alone."

She looked at me surprised, slightly disconcerted. "Okay," she said.

I slept little that night, and the next night, and the night after that. When I did sleep it was fitful and unrefreshing. I kept hearing the voice: "Peter, there is more to life.…" I couldn't get it out of my head. "Peter, there is more.…" Even when I prayed I kept hearing the words: "There is more.…"

Of one thing I was certain: It wasn't a human voice. It was God's voice speaking to me: "Peter, there is more to life than this."

I still didn't say anything to anybody, not even to Joan, because what would she say? That I was just imagining this? That I was having a nightmare? Or worse, that I was delusional? That I needed psychiatric help?

A week passed. That Sunday at church I felt unsettled in my soul, in the deepest part of me. Another week passed. After we came home from church the second Sunday I came close to telling her about the voice, but I chickened out.

Finally, on the Tuesday before Thanksgiving, I said to her, "Honey, it's a beautiful day. Why don't we pack a lunch and have a picnic?"

"Where?" she asked.

"Out in the orange groves. There's a park on the Caloosahatchee River.

It's about an hour from here, on the road to Lake Okeechobee."

"That's a wonderful idea," she said.

We packed our lunch in the kitchen—ham and cheese sandwiches, two slices of apple pie, and a quart of orange juice left over from breakfast.

Joan handed me a table cloth. "Here, slip this into the basket," she said, "unless you want to eat off a dirty picnic table."

Silently, I did what I was told.

"Honey, you've been awfully quiet today," she said. "Come to think of it, you've been awfully quiet the past several days. Everything is all right, isn't it?"

I mumbled an acknowledgment but really didn't answer her. It had been two weeks since I heard the voice, and for two weeks I had been silent on the subject.

Our drive to the park was just as quiet. My stomach was in knots. When we reached Telegraph Creek, I knew the park lay just ahead. I wheeled into a clearing where we spotted an empty picnic table. We took the basket out of the trunk and spread out the table cloth.

All the while neither of us said a word. By now, I thought, Joan had to know that something was wrong. The stillness was broken by two noisy scrub jays in furious pursuit of one another. I wondered if that might be some kind of omen.

After we sat down, I looked at Joan across the table as she bowed her head. When she finished praying, I took a deep breath. "Honey," I said, barely able to get the words out. "Honey, there's something I have to tell you."

She looked at me with the expression of someone anticipating some horrible revelation. What was she expecting me to tell her? That I had robbed a bank? That I had some incurable disease? That I had been unfaithful to her?

When I told her about the voice, her response was unlike anything I had ever imagined. Not in my wildest dreams would I have anticipated it. But it was a response that would change the rest of our lives.

Chapter Two

'Please God, Don't Let Leonard Die'

B ack in 1935 there was a popular George Marshall movie starring Will Rogers called "Life Begins at Forty." My answer to that is a song from the George and Ira Gershwin opera *Porgy and Bess* that came out the same year. The title of that song was "It Ain't Necessarily So."

For me, life began at sixty-seven. But spiritual journeys seldom begin at a specific moment. Mine didn't begin when I heard the voice on the boat any more than the Apostle Paul's journey began when he encountered a blinding light on the Damascus road. There's usually a lot that goes on beforehand, things that happen in one's life that foreshadow what's to come. I think of my life—the first sixty-seven years—as a prelude to a choral symphony, as a build-up to the real thing. And so before I reveal what Joan said to me after I told her about the voice, I begin my story where my spiritual journey began—in rural Minnesota.

I was born on the twelfth of June, 1923, the eleventh of twelve children on a farm outside of Leota, a little town in the southwest corner of the state. As a child my father, Peter John, had moved there from Michigan when his father acquired a section of undeveloped land under the Homestead Act of 1862, which President Lincoln signed into law. The deal was that my grandfather would promise to cultivate the land and live on it for five years. That's what attracted so many people to the western states in those days. Old Abe knew what he was doing, and he had the Civil War to cope with on top of that!

In 1900 my father, who eventually took over the homestead from my grandfather, married Jenny Eckhoff, who was to become my mother. She herself had grown up on a farm in Illinois. She bore her twelve children over a twenty-three year period, raising half of them during the Great Depression. A beautiful woman in every way and a wonderful mom, she was a master at disciplining her children, doing so with grace and wisdom and God-like love.

She taught not by precept but by example. I had just turned ten when the first Big Drought struck in the summer of 1933. Miserable dust storms swept through the Minnesota prairies, turning days into nights and the ground into granite. Swarms of flies pelted the screens of our kitchen porch. We had no fans, no electricity, no running water. The chickens poked around the yard with their beaks wide open, it was that hot.

One blistering day in July my father and older brothers were out in the field. My mother was in the kitchen working at the stove, getting dinner ready for the family, sweat pouring down her face. "Peter," she said, "would you water the chickens, please?"

That meant I would have to carry two pails from the kitchen porch to the windmill at the far end of the yard, fill them with water, carry the water back to the chickens, and pour it into their dishes. That was hard work, especially on a 95-degree day.

"Why?" I replied.

Mother looked at me, astonished. Without saying a word, she stopped what she was doing, walked over to the kitchen porch, and picked up the pails.

"Oh brother," I muttered to myself, "what do I do now?"

I followed her meekly across the farmyard to the windmill where she began pumping the water into the pails. I grabbed the pump handle. She took my hand and gently moved it away. I began to cry. She filled both pails, carried them to the chickens, and dispensed the water into the dishes—all without saying a word. Then she handed me the empty pails and said quietly, "Now you may take these back to the house."

It was a lesson I never forgot.

❧ ❧ ❧

Before I started school we moved to a farm outside Edgerton where my father rented a half section of land. Carting our belongings in a horse-drawn wagon, we must have looked like the Joads in *The Grapes of Wrath*. I sat on top with my mother and two-year-old sister, Jeneva, while the others followed on horseback.

My father worked from sunup to sundown. My older siblings helped with the planting and harvest and the endless chores. Our crops consisted of oats and corn and flax. My father owned twenty-seven head of cattle— mostly Holstein.

After we settled into the new farm, we took in a German shepherd from a neighboring farm. We named him Tike. Affectionate, frisky and eager to please, Tike instantly won his way into our hearts.

Although twenty-three years separated my oldest brother, John, and my youngest sister, Jeneva—a not uncommon phenomenon among farm families in those days—we were an uncommonly close-knit family. I was especially close to my brother Leonard, a twin of my brother Hank. We were four years apart in age but had many things in common including a lust for adventure and a penchant for making play out of work. Often we'd round up the cattle together, riding bareback on the horses, while Tike, who had a similar penchant for play, would make a game out of rounding up the cattle. If a cow wandered out of the herd, Tike would take off like a dart, prance sideways as he approached the cow, and clamp his jaw on the cow's tail, tugging it back to the herd. Tike snapped off more than one tail that way, and the cows had grown leery of him. My father even had the vet file his teeth down so he couldn't snap off any more tails.

Leonard and I could get rambunctious. Once we were riding our bikes in town, seeing what tricks we could do.

"Look, no hands!" called Leonard. Both his hands were thrust towards the sky as he pedaled furiously. He skidded to a stop, turned around and looked at me as if to challenge me.

I couldn't resist; I wanted to see if I could do the same. Pointing myself in his direction, I worked up a bit of speed and let go of the handlebars. The front wheel swung to the side and I went sprawling toward a brick wall. I threw out my right hand to break my fall and scraped it against the wall.

At home my mother cleaned the wound as best she could and bandaged it up. "Looks like it's going to be okay," she said. Years later, when I joined the Army Air Corps, it became a major medical problem.

Sometimes there were more serious problems. One day I was out in the fields doing my chores. My father was pitching hay. As a father of twelve children, he had a lot on his mind and sometimes got on edge. He mentioned something he was angry about and I, being a boisterous kid, didn't react in a way he thought appropriate.

He threw the pitchfork at me like a spear and I ducked. I hate to think what would have happened if I hadn't ducked.

I ran off into the cornfields and spent the night huddled on the ground. In the morning I came back and without a word resumed my chores where I had left off the previous afternoon.

My mother was worried sick. When I didn't come home, my father told her what happened. They had a close relationship, and he could confess things like that to her. To me, though, he said nothing.

❄❄ ❄❄ ❄❄

It was late in the afternoon on the ninth of May, 1933. Leonard said, "Come on, Pete. It's time to get the cows." He jumped on his horse, and I jumped on mine. We spotted the herd a quarter mile ahead of us. Then Leonard said, "Come on, Pete, let's race."

As we galloped toward the herd with Tike at our side, one of the cows bolted. Instantly, Tike took off after the cow and got it into full gallop, steering it right at Leonard's horse. My heart stopped as the two collided. Leonard flew over the animals and landed headfirst on the ground with a cracking sound. The horses drew to a halt. I dropped my lines and ran over to my brother.

"Oh God, help us!" I cried as I looked at his face. Foam oozed out of his nose and ears. His head was shattered. "Leonard, Leonard!" I cried. I was vaguely aware that Tike was circling clockwise while the cows gazed at us from outside the perimeter.

Back in the farmyard, my father and my brothers Tom and Hank took notice of the scene and rushed out in the car. Meanwhile I knelt over my brother and for the first time in my life prayed to God in earnest: "Please, God, don't let Leonard die...please... please...." Before, whenever I prayed, the words had been someone else's—"Now I lay me down to sleep"—and spoken by rote. But now, for the first time, I was using my own words, pleading to God from my heart.

My father and brothers lifted Leonard up from the ground and laid him across the backseat of the car. I ran back to the farmhouse to get my mother. A half hour later, at our family doctor's office in Edgerton, we anxiously waited for Dr. Beckering to say something—anything—as he examined my brother who lay motionless on the table. He lifted Leonard's eyelids and checked his pupils. Then he spoke the dreaded words: "I'm sorry." Through the sobbing I heard him say something about a cerebral hemorrhage, but it didn't matter. Leonard was gone.

My family was devastated. I remember listening at the door of my brother's room while my mother cried, "Dear Leonard, my dear Leonard." I remember seeing my father go out behind the tool shed near the barn and come back fifteen minutes later with his eyes all watery and red. For months, he insisted on holding Leonard's place at the dinner table.

I remember questioning God. Why did he do this? Why did he take Leonard away? Why did he let this happen if he loved us? I kept asking questions but never got a satisfactory answer. It didn't make it any easier when my father took our precious dog, Tike, out behind the tool shed and shot him.

My parents' faith had to be shaken as much as mine, although they never expressed it in so many words. What I had learned in church and Sunday School was that everything happened for a reason, that nothing happened without God's will. The minister even said that at Leonard's funeral.

But in my ten-year-old mind it made no sense, no sense at all. All I knew was that Leonard was dead and he wasn't coming back.

Chapter Three

'Apology Accepted'

I f large families were the custom of the day, so was the pitching in of neighbors to help anyone in need. The night Leonard died, our three neighbors—the Kuypers, the Rooses, and the Haitsmas—milked the cows, fed the chickens, and prepared the dinner for our huge family.

In my mind's eye I can still see Mrs. Roos working over my mother's stove and turning to embrace her when we returned from Dr. Beckering's office in Edgerton.

They were wonderful people, our neighbors, but there was something different about the Haitsmas' son, Heine. He was the school bully. We had a one-room school at the far edge of the farm, a clapboard building that housed twenty-five to thirty children in all eight grades. In the spring of 1934, my younger sister Jeneva and I were the last from our family to go to that school. She was in the third grade and I was in the fifth, one of three pupils in my class. Heine was in the eighth grade and the biggest kid in the room. Already fourteen, he was at an age when the male hormones typically start kicking in, but I was too young to know about those things then.

All I knew was that I hated him. Whenever Jeneva and I walked home from school, Heine would come up from behind and start harassing us. Sometimes he would do it with words; sometimes he would pull off Jeneva's hat and grab her pigtails.

In early April, the first thaw of spring had set in. Jeneva and I edged our way home along the road, taking care not to slip into the mud. Before either of us knew it, Heine had crept up from behind. He hooked Jeneva's ankle with his foot, and propelled her into the mud.

Jeneva shrieked and hit the mud with a splatter. I helped her up and shouted at Heine to go away. Since he was too big for me, I couldn't fight back. I felt angry and humiliated.

As soon as we got home, I went straight to the tool shed, grabbed a broken pitchfork, and clamped the handle in a vice. I sawed a nine-inch length off the handle. Then I drove a nail into the end, sawed off the head, and filed it down until it was razor-sharp.

My plan was to smuggle the weapon to school the next day in my lunch box. I had vowed that if Heine came after my sister again I was going to stab him with it.

By the grace of God, my brother Tom—seven years older than I—caught me filing the nail. "What on earth are you doing?" he said.

I told him.

"Give it to me right now!" he demanded. He clamped the nail in the vice and yanked it out of the handle. "Tomorrow," he said, "I'm going to wait for you and Jeneva when you come home from school."

The next day Tom waited out by the road, pretending to be mending a fencepost. Jeneva and I passed by, then Heine. Tom grabbed Heine by the collar, pulled his face up to his, and said in a low voice: "Listen, if you ever touch my sister or brother again, you'll have to deal with me. Understand?"

Heine never bothered us after that.

In the summer of 1965, I decided to go back to Edgerton for the town's big Fourth of July celebration. The event had always been a highlight of my childhood and I wanted to recapture the experience as an adult. I still had siblings in the area including an older sister, Elizabeth.

I set my folding chair next to Elizabeth's in front of Hartog's department store, waiting for the parade to begin. A few minutes later a man in his mid-forties approached us from across the road and called my name: "Pete? Pete VandenBosch?"

I looked up.

"Heine Haitsma," he said, extending his hand.

The moment he introduced himself, the image of my little sister Jeneva being hurled into the mud sprang into my mind, then the sawed-off pitchfork handle with the nail sticking out of the end.

"Pete," the man said again. "I'm Heine, remember me?"

I stood up and took his hand but said nothing.

"I just want to say I'm sorry for the way I treated you and your sister," he said.

"Heine," I said, "you were fourteen years old. That was a long time ago."

"I know," he said. "But there was no excuse for what I did, and I apologize."

After hesitating I said, "Apology accepted."

Elizabeth, still seated in her folding chair, looked up at me and smiled. "I wish Jeneva could hear you two talking," she said.

"Jeneva…where is she?" Heine asked.

I explained that Jeneva was living in California, was married with five children and doing well.

"Well, I'm glad to hear that," Heine said. "Please convey my apology to her too, and wish her well for me, would you please?"

We shook hands again. Then he turned and disappeared across the road.

Although the incident involving Heine Haitsma and my sister had happened so many years ago, I had never really put it out of my mind. Yet when Heine offered his apology and I accepted, I felt the weight of an old grudge lifted from my shoulders. Is it better to forgive or to be forgiven? It would still take me a while to find the answer.

Chapter Four

Leaving Home

I f there's one thing that sets us humans apart from other creatures on this planet, it's that we're spiritual beings. Our aim isn't merely to survive but to find meaning in our lives. "Why are we here?" is a question only humans are capable of asking themselves. If we're fortunate enough to find the answer, our next step is to act on it.

For me the answer came in two defining moments—call them epiphanies—that I experienced in my childhood. Each foretold something that was to give meaning and purpose to my life.

The first one had to do with music. As far back as I can remember, music was part of my life. When I was a kid, a neighbor had given my father a broken cylinder player with a hand-crank. After he got it to work, he gave it to me along with a half-dozen cylinders with choral music. I played the cylinders in the corn crib, imagining myself directing a great choir in front of a great audience. I played them over and over until they got so scratchy I could barely make out the music.

When I was twelve, our minister announced that the Calvin College *a cappella* glee club was coming to town. They were coming all the way from Grand Rapids, Michigan, to sing at the Edgerton Christian Reformed Church. My father insisted we go early so we'd get seats near the front. The Glee Club was directed by the renowned Professor Seymour Swets.

The sanctuary was packed, but we managed to squeeze in about six rows back. I sat transfixed through the concert while Professor Swets led the glee club through their repertoire. Their last number was "A Mighty Fortress

Is Our God," an eight-part harmony arranged by Carl Muller, whose name I came to know much later. It was awesome! As the song built to a climax, my twelve-year-old soul was ready to leave this world. Afterwards, I said to my dad, "I want to see Professor Swets."

"Oh, he won't have time to see you," he said.

"But I've got to see him," I insisted. I glanced at the rear of the sanctuary where the choir was disrobing. There I spotted Professor Swets. I shoved my way to the back and tugged at his sleeve.

"Professor Swets?" I said.

He turned to look at me.

"I'm Peter VandenBosch. I want to be a conductor just like you some day. Can you tell me how to go about it?"

"Please excuse my son," interrupted my mother, catching up with me. "He can be pretty bold sometimes."

"Oh, no matter," Professor Swets said. Then he put his hand on my shoulder. "Young man," he said, "give your life to the Lord. Ask him to lead you and he will show you the way."

My encounter with Professor Swets couldn't have lasted more than a minute, but it has stayed with me to this day.

My second epiphany had to do with flight. It was a late afternoon in August 1936, in the middle of another bone-dry summer. We had a haystack out behind the barn where my younger sister Jeneva and I would spend time yakking and making plans for the future. Usually those plans didn't entail staying on the farm. Sometimes she'd make sandwiches while I finished the morning chores. Then we'd meet at the haystack for lunch. One day I showed up late at the appointed spot. Jeneva was impatient. "Here, eat your sandwich. It's getting stale."

Taking the sandwich, I fell into the base of the haystack and laid my head back in the straw. A faint rumble sounded in the distance. "Must be a thunderstorm coming up," I said.

"Don't you wish. There isn't a cloud in sight," Jeneva said.

"Then it must be a threshing machine at the Roos's farm."

A few seconds later I realized the rumble wasn't coming from our neighbor's farm, let alone from ground level. Rather, it was coming from the sky and getting louder. I got to my feet, looked up, and spotted a three-engine plane approaching from the southwest.

"Just look that that!" I exclaimed to my sister. "A Ford Tri-Motor. I read about it in *Collier's*."

"Must be out of Sioux Falls," she ventured.

"It has to be. It's the only commercial airport around. Did you know there are only two-hundred of those airplanes? The 'Tin Goose' they call it."

"You seem to know an awful lot about it. Wonder where it's going."

"Minneapolis, I bet." I fixed my gaze on the plane, wondering what it would be like to sit at the controls of that magnificent flying machine. "Just wait and see, Jeneva. One day I'm going to fly one of those."

As I watched the plane disappear, my father came out from the barn, spotted my sister and me at the haystack, and shouted, "Hey, Peter, get your head out of the sky! Don't you know you have cows to milk? And Jeneva, get inside and help your mother!"

Notwithstanding my father's agitation—after all, he had a farm to look after and a big family to feed—my sighting of that Ford Tri-Motor proved to be another defining moment in my life.

꒰ꔛ꒱ ꒰ꔛ꒱ ꒰ꔛ꒱

One by one my brothers left the farm. John, twenty-one years my senior, had taken a teaching and choir directing position at Western Christian High School in Hull, Iowa. Tom, seven years older than I, moved to Bellflower, California, where he started a hay-hauling business. Gerrit, another older brother, moved to Grand Rapids, Michigan, and started a business grinding coffee and selling it door-to-door.

In Minnesota in those days you were liable to wind up in jail if you left home before the age of twenty-one. For my brother Hank, Leonard's surviving twin, twenty-one couldn't come soon enough. On his twenty-first birthday, he packed up his belongings, hopped in his car, and followed Gerrit to Michigan.

That left me, the youngest son in a family of eleven children, to carry on the farm. But I was no more interested in farming than my brothers were. When I was seventeen, the summer before my senior year in high school, my father took me aside and said, "Peter, I've been thinking about you and your future. I see you've been keeping company with Ruth, that nice young woman in your Sunday School class.

"I have a proposition," he continued. "If you work for me from the time you graduate from high school until you're twenty-one, you and your new wife can live in this house—I will build a new one for Mom and me—and then you can take over the farm. Not only that, you'll have all the chickens and cattle and machinery you'll need."

I couldn't believe my father's generous offer. If I accepted, not only would my future be secure, but I'd be launched into instant wealth. The next Saturday, at breakfast, he announced that he was going to Sioux Falls to check out a tractor.

"I'll be back in time for supper," he said. "Peter, you're in charge of the milking."

As soon as my father disappeared through the screen door, Mother took me aside and said, "Peter, please come with me." I followed her into the master bedroom. "Here," she said, motioning to the floor. "Kneel down beside the bed. I'm going to kneel down on the other side." After we knelt, she reached for my hands across the bed and said, "Peter, it's time to lay your life in front of the Lord." Then she prayed: "Dear God, guide Peter to make the decision that will please you in his life."

That was it, no sermon, no lecture, nothing. Never again did she bring up the subject. The decision was the most important of my life, and it was mine alone to make.

That fall I started my senior year at Western Christian High School in Hull, Iowa, sixty miles down the road from Edgertown. I would spend my weekdays in Hull, which I had been doing since my freshman year, boarding at local homes. On weekends I would make the trip back and forth in a 1929 Model A that my father had allowed me to purchase. Four or five other kids from Edgerton usually rode along.

By the time I started at Western Christian, John had been promoted to principal. Even though he was my brother, in school I had to call him "Mr. VandenBosch." After he became principal, he continued to direct the school choir.

Thanks to Professor Swets, I was set on a career in music—choral directing, singing, anything. I knew I had the talent for it. I was the best tenor in the Western Christian choir. Now and then my brother would even assign me a solo part.

But I was totally unprepared for what happened in rehearsal one afternoon. John was at the director's podium drilling the choir on a piece that was giving us difficulty. A teacher came into the room and whispered in his ear. My brother turned to me and said, "Peter!"

"Yes, Mr. VandenBosch," I responded.

"Come to the podium. I want you to take over." He handed me his baton and left the room.

I stood at the podium and faced my schoolmates. At first I thought they might chuckle or laugh, but nobody did. They simply waited for me to continue the number. I turned to the accompanist. She was waiting too.

With no warm up, no preparation whatsoever, I was holding a baton in my hand and facing a real live choir. When my brother returned fifteen minutes later, he had the choir run through the piece one more time with me directing. When we finished, he nodded at me and said, "Not bad. Not bad at all."

A month later my brother called me out of the classroom into his office. I was apprehensive. Had I done something wrong?

"Peter," he said, "I got this request from a group of men here in Hull. They're putting together an octet and want someone to direct them. I can't do it. Will you do it? I want to tell them that you'll do it."

"What does a director do?"

"Well, you know from when you took over for me."

"But that was for one song."

"Look, it isn't that difficult. Do exactly what you did before. Just listen. When they sing the wrong notes or the tempo is off, have them do it over. If the blend isn't right, move them around. Have them adopt a style that's pleasing to your ear."

"Well, I think I can do that."

"Good," he said. "I'll call and tell them you'll do it."

The very next evening I found myself in the first rehearsal of the Hull Men's Octet—eight men in their twenties and thirties. Here I was, a seventeen-year-old upstart from another town. But they didn't treat me like a stranger or even as an inferior. At first I sat and listened to them. Then I got up and started directing. I taught them how to sing vowels—just as my brother did with the school choir—and moved them around until the blend sounded just right.

In March 1941—three months short of my eighteenth birthday—the Hull Men's Octet sang at the Christian Reformed Church in Sheldon, Iowa. That was my debut as a choral conductor.

But as graduation approached I knew I had to make a decision about my father's offer. My brother John had just accepted a new job as principal of a Christian high school in Muskegon, Michigan. He would be the third of my brothers, after Gerrit and Hank, to move to that state. What should I do? Accept my father's offer and stay on the farm? Follow my brothers to Michigan?

Gerrit and his wife, Sadie, had recently bought a house in Grand Rapids to accommodate their growing family. He offered to take me in until I found a job and could live on my own. That sounded pretty good. Moreover, the State of Minnesota had lowered the age when a child could legally leave home from twenty-one to eighteen. Ever since my father made his offer, I had been putting off telling him what I wanted to do. And my eighteenth birthday was coming up in June.

"Well, Peter," he said finally, drawing a chair to the kitchen table. "Have you decided what you want to do yet?"

I took a deep breath and said, "I have."

When I told him about my plan, his eyes welled up with tears. I could feel his heart break when I told him, "Dad, I just don't want to stay on the farm." For several minutes we sat at the table in silence. I couldn't look at him.

Finally he said, "Come with me." I followed him into the master bedroom, the holy of holies where my mother had taken me months before to ask for God's guidance.

"Here, sit on the bed," he said, seating himself by the window. In front of the window, on a pedestal table, stood a long-necked telephone.

"Peter," he said. "You may go to Michigan. I can't hold you back any more than I could your brothers. Your mother and I knew what your answer was going to be, but I had to hear it from you. So go ahead and pack your clothes. John will be here tomorrow to pick you up."

My father reached for his wallet and withdrew ten one-dollar bills. "Here, this is for you," he said. "Just remember one thing." He motioned to the telephone silhouetted against the window. "Don't ever call me for money. From now on, you're on your own."

The next morning, on my eighteenth birthday, John arrived in his car to pick me up. The three remaining members of my family—my parents and little sister Jeneva—came out of the house to see us off. Father gripped my hand; he was too choked up to speak. Mother gave me a long hug and said, "God be with you, Peter." When I turned to Jeneva, she threw her arms around me and burst back to the house sobbing.

I got into the car with John. "Here's three dollars for gas," I said, handing him the money. I had seven dollars left. When I waved my last good bye through the car window, I knew that I was on own, just like my father said.

But as determined as I was to make him proud of me, I couldn't have imagined what lay ahead.

Chapter Five

Yearning to Fly

I should have known what my father would do after I left home. Whenever I thought of him shooting Tike, our German shepherd, after Leonard died, that might have given me a clue. What he did this time was just as impulsive; He upped and sold the farm. In retrospect, had he waited another year or two after the Depression, he could have doubled his money. But what was done was done. He and Mother retired to a house in Edgerton. Eventually, Jeneva, the last of the children to leave home, got married and moved to California.

Meanwhile I moved in with my brother Gerrit and his family in Grand Rapids. In many ways Grand Rapids was like Edgerton but on a larger scale. The city, the second largest in Michigan, boasted a population of 164,000—mainly people of Dutch Calvinist descent who went to church on Sunday and worked hard and voted Republican. Surrounding woodlands and an abundant supply of water power from the Grand River had transformed the city from a logging backwater in the mid-1800s into the country's premier furniture-producing center.

Grand Rapids valued entrepreneurship as much as a strong work ethic, and Gerrit fit in perfectly. He ran his own business called the Star Coffee Company. Every morning at 6 o'clock he would begin the day by grinding coffee in his basement. He'd measure it all very carefully and grind it up and put it in paper bags. Then at 8 o'clock sharp he'd set out in his van and peddle the stuff door-to-door. He called it his secret blend.

The enterprise didn't make him rich, but it did support his family. As for supporting myself, I knew it was sink or swim, and all I had in my pocket was the seven dollars left over from my father. As soon as I moved in with Gerrit, I picked up a *Grand Rapids Press* for five cents, searched the classified ads, and circled one that said "Help Wanted: Dishwasher" at Woolworth's five-and-dime store. Armed with directions from my sister-in-law, Sadie, I hopped a bus downtown to Campau Square where the store was located. The trip cost another five cents. I sought out the manager who handed me an application which I duly filled out. After he looked it over, he said, "When can you start?"

"Right now," I said.

"The job pays twenty cents an hour."

Immediately I set to work. I couldn't believe my good fortune. By the end of the first hour, I had not only recovered the cost of my job search, I had increased my assets to seven dollars and ten cents.

Soon enough I realized that twenty cents an hour didn't go very far in Grand Rapids. A few months later I got a better-paying job at Irwin Seating Company on Buchanan Avenue, cutting patterns for seat cushions. But I still wasn't making enough to live on my own. Finally, Gerrit took me aside and said, "Look, you ought to get a job with Bell Telephone. They're putting up new telephone poles in town—I see them every day on my rounds. You'd fit with your farm experience."

At first I resisted—heavy manual labor wasn't high on my career list—but Gerrit kept pushing. When he asked a worker how much the job paid—seventy-five cents an hour!—I was suddenly eager to apply. Once again, I hopped on a bus in hopes of securing a job interview, but alas, there were no openings. I went back a second time, and a third. Two or three times a week I went back until the man in the employment office said, "You really want a job here, don't you?"

"Yes, sir, I do!" I said.

"Well, an opening just came up."

My persistence, aided by a bit of fortuitous timing, finally paid off. The next morning I reported to my new job site. Even though a machine did most of the work, drilling ten-foot holes in the ground and dropping fifty-foot telephone poles in them was a strenuous undertaking, even for a strapping eighteen-year-old. But as Gerrit said, my farm experience made me a good fit.

Before long I managed to scrape together enough money to begin dating a young woman I had become interested in. We had met at a place where every good Christian mother hopes her son might meet a prospective wife; at church. In my case it was the East Leonard Christian Reformed Church, which I attended with Gerrit and his family.

No sooner had my financial and romantic prospects begun to improve when something happened that changed everything. Sunday, December 7, dawned cloudy and cold with a dust of snow on the ground. My girlfriend's aunt and uncle had invited us over for dinner after church. After we finished eating we reconvened in the living room for coffee. Her uncle turned on the radio to check the progress of a football game. It was playoff season, and the New York Giants had just scored a touchdown. The cheering stopped as the radio fell silent. A few seconds later an announcer came on. "Ladies and Gentlemen," he said. "We interrupt this broadcast to bring you an important bulletin....Washington: The White House announces an attack on Pearl Harbor."

The news came at exactly 2:26 p.m. In Honolulu it was 9:26 in the morning. We listened in stunned silence as details of the Japanese attack came in. By nightfall the full extent of the devastation became known: two hundred planes destroyed, twenty-three hundred Americans killed, the U.S.S. Arizona and seven other navy ships torpedoed and sunk.

The next morning President Franklin Roosevelt called an emergency session of Congress. We listened again as the president, declaring the attack a date that would live in infamy, called for Congress to declare war on Japan.

Two days later, Germany and Italy declared war on the United States. All of a sudden my country, which was minding its own business and valued peace above everything else, found itself at war in two different parts of the world. We weren't prepared for war, we didn't want war, we didn't believe in war. But the Japanese invasion and the declaration of war by Germany and Italy changed that overnight.

Like every red-blooded American male of fighting age, I rushed to enlist in the war effort. When I arrived at the federal building on Pearl Street, the line was two-and-a-half blocks long. I took my place at the rear and waited for three hours. Once inside the door, I waited another hour. When I finally reached the head of the line, the enlistment officer, without so much as raising his eyes, asked me to verify my name, address and date and place of birth on the form in front of him. Then he said, "What service to you want to enlist for?"

"Army Air Corps," I said. From the moment I had spotted that Ford Tri-Motor over my father's farm, I had yearned to fly an airplane. Now was my big chance. Not only did I want to serve my country, I wanted to do it at the controls of a P-38 Lightning. With enormous twin booms and counter-rotating props, it was the best twin-engine fighter plane ever built. When I saw one for the first time at the Kent County Airport in Grand Rapids, I knew at once that the P-38 Lightning, not the Ford Tri-Motor, was the plane I wanted to fly.

Returning to my brother's home, I waited for the phone to ring, thinking it might be a day or two. I waited, and waited. The days turned into weeks, the weeks turned into months. Eventually I gave up on getting a phone call. Every afternoon, after returning from work, I checked the mail box for a letter from the Army Air Corps. But none came.

Meanwhile Bell Telephone notified me that my job would be waiting for me when I came back from the service. That somehow assured me that my time to be called for duty would eventually come. And it gave me a sense of security to know I would be employed when the war was over. So I broached to my girlfriend, without exactly proposing to her, the idea of getting married. My mother wasn't keen on the idea, but I didn't know whether her objection had to do with the woman I was dating or the fact that I was about to go off to war.

Finally, in January 1943, the much-anticipated letter arrived. I was ecstatic. Nobody was more prepared to go to war for his country—as the pilot of a P-38 Lightning—than I was. The letter instructed me to report to the federal building on Pearl Street. With forty other enlistees, I boarded a bus for Detroit. At Detroit's Union Station we joined several hundred more enlistees waiting to board the train. Our destination; Miami Beach.

The Atlantic Towers, a six-story hotel overlooking the ocean, wasn't your typical boot camp. The Army had commandeered the building and surrounding grounds for use as a training center for Air Corps cadets. In basic training we spent hours each day exercising and marching in step. It didn't matter if you were five-feet-six or six-feet-five, you had to march in step. Most important, we learned there were three ways of doing things: the right way, the wrong way, and the Army way.

Our next orders were to report to Kent State University in Ohio for flight instruction. Our group arrived by train and began attending classes on the university campus. Every day I felt I was getting closer to my goal of piloting the P-38 Lightning.

During my training at Kent State, two important things happened. First, I got married to the young lady I had been dating. My mother had said to me, "Peter, are you sure you have the right one?" But I didn't listen to her. The pressures on young men going into the service were enormous. Knowing that your chances of survival were not that great caused you to make decisions you wouldn't have otherwise. In retrospect—how much easier it is to see things that way—I shouldn't have gotten married when I did. I should have waited until after the war and gone to college first. But I was more interested in having a family.

The second thing that happened to me had consequences no less devastating than marrying the wrong woman at the wrong time. In flight training I developed a fungus on my right hand, the delayed result of having scraped it against the brick wall back in Edgerton when I was doing bicycle stunts with my brother Leonard. Some bacteria seized the opportunity to lodge under the skin and slept there like Rip Van Winkle for the next decade.

The bacteria lay dormant until the hot, moist heat of Miami Beach caused it to stir. By the time I reached Kent State it exploded. Whenever I made a fist, blood and puss oozed out between my swollen fingers. Before long, my fingernails rotted off.

The Army sent me to the Cleveland Clinic where the doctors got the swelling down. They told me to keep my hand wrapped in gauze and ointment. That helped a little, but the fungus didn't go away.

That fall when I arrived at my next training venue—the Army Air Corps base in San Antonio—the Texas heat exploded it all over again. I went to see the commanding officer and told him I didn't think I was getting the right treatment. When he looked at my hand, he almost flipped out of his chair. "I'm taking you off active status!" he said. "You're going to have that thing looked at right now."

When I left his office I found myself in the examination room at the base hospital. Again a team of doctors gathered to have a look. Unraveling the gauze to show them my hand, I heard a chorus of "hmms" and one of them said something about experimental treatment. But all I could think of was, how long would I be stuck here? How long would I be on inactive status? How long would I have to wait to fly?

I sought out the hospital chaplain, a Major Miller, for consolation.

"Of course you want to fly—who doesn't at this base?" he said. "But from the looks of your hand, I think you'll be grounded for a while." After he let that sink in for a few seconds, he said, "Do you have any other interests?"

"Besides flying?"

"Besides flying."

My mind flashed back to my brother John's rehearsal room at the Christian School in Hull, Iowa. "Well, I like to sing," I said. "And I did some choral directing in high school. Why?"

"Well," he said, "we have a bunch of nurses here—about twenty of them—who want to put on a Christmas concert for the troops. They need someone to direct them, but I don't have the time."

I thought of my brother John again, asking me to direct the men's octet back in Hull. My heart picked up a few beats while I waited for the chaplain to continue speaking.

"Would you be interested in taking my place?" he said.

"Would I be interested! When's the next rehearsal?"

"As soon as you get out of here."

"I'll do it!"

"Another thing," he continued. "You said you like to sing. What are you, a tenor?"

"Second tenor," I said.

The chaplain fell silent again, as if lost in thought. Finally he said, "May I ask you a personal question?"

"That depends on how personal. What is it?"

"Do you believe in providence?"

"That *is* a personal question," I said. I thought of my minister back in Edgerton who said that God had a plan for everyone, but I had a hard time believing that after Leonard died. "Why do you ask?"

"Well, you said your other passion was music."

"You wanted to know if I had other *interests*, but yeah, I can be passionate about music."

"That's where providence comes in. I think God has a plan for you."

Not him too! I thought. Do all men-of-the-cloth think the same way? "What are you getting at?" I asked.

"There's a men's octet here that sings on Armed Forces Radio. Their second tenor just shipped out to the Pacific. They need someone to replace him. Why don't you try out?"

So maybe *that* was God's plan for me. When all was said and done, not only was I put in charge of the nurses choir, but I passed my audition for the Army Air Corps Octet. Suddenly I found myself in the company of singers from Fred Waring's outfit and Andrew Gainey, the famous baritone from the Metropolitan Opera. Every Friday night we did a half-hour program on Armed Forces Radio.

If that was God's plan, it didn't end there. One of the singers in the octet was a Captain Harrison, a doctor. One day at rehearsal I showed him my hand.

"You know, there's a brand new treatment for this sort of thing," he said. "It's still experimental, but I think it will work."

When I called home the next day, my father was skeptical. "Radiation! I never heard of such a thing," he exclaimed. "Look, I know our congressman, August Andresen. I want to talk to him about this radiation treatment—you say it's experimental?—because if it causes terrible things to happen, I want to make sure the army takes care of you."

Somehow I managed to get through the nurses' concert directing with an infected hand. A few weeks later my father called with a belated Christmas present; Congressman Andresen had assured him that if I reacted adversely to the radiation, the army would indeed "take care" of me.

The radiation worked. Within weeks my hand cleared up. At last I was going to realize my dream of flying the P-38 Lightning! Six months after reporting to San Antonio, I was finally assigned to a flight training class of one hundred and seventy-nine pilots. Of that number, fifty would be chosen to fly.

The moment the names were posted on the base bulletin board, I rushed out to check the list. But my name wasn't on it. I looked again and didn't find it. Once more I looked; nothing. My eyes glazed over. My head went into a spin. Gradually it dawned on me that I wasn't among the fifty chosen to fly. Instead, I was among the one hundred and twenty-nine rejects who would be given something else to do.

Was *that* God's plan for me? Or was it his idea of a joke? I went behind the barracks—out of sight of everyone else on the base—and cried like a baby.

Chapter Six

The Wings of War

After my tears dried I took stock of my options. I had two choices: Either I could become a flight engineer, or I could become a radio operator-gunner. Choosing the latter, I got transferred to an Air Corps training school in Sioux Falls, South Dakota—fifty miles from the farm where I had grown up—to be trained as a radio operator.

Other than my Friday night slot on Armed Forces Radio, I'd had no experience in radio, but that didn't stop me. In Sioux Falls I learned the Morse Code and sailed through all my classes.

My next stop was Yuma, Arizona—the Air Corps gunnery school. I found that pretty easy, too. Having abandoned my goal of fighting the war from the cockpit of a P-38 Lighting, I was learning how to do it from the controls of a radio transmitter and the crosshairs of a gun scope. What mattered was winning the war.

After gunnery school it was on to Boise, Idaho, where I met my flight crew, most of them fresh out of training like me. They included A. E. "Sandy" Sanders, our captain; Giles Gorham, the co-captain; Troy Shields, the tail gunner; Bill Bruton, the ball gunner; Tommy Lutz, the nose gunner; Roy Heffner, the navigator; George Haviland, the bombardier, and me, the radio operator.

Whether it was meant to be or whether it just happened, we became the best of buddies. Bill Bruton, the ball gunner, had grown up in rural Texas, and for hours we would swap stories about our childhood years on the farm and talk about getting out and seeing the world, even if it meant looking at it through the bay doors of a bomber.

Mostly we talked about the war. In the back of our minds there was always the question: Will I make it back alive? But that was something we kept to ourselves; we didn't want anybody to know how scared we were. Three years had passed since the Japanese bombed Pearl Harbor—it was December of 1944 already—and rumors of German defections were drifting in from the Western Front.

After a few months of training together, we boarded the overnight train to Lincoln, Nebraska to meet our plane. Somewhere between Boise and Lincoln—six thousand miles from the Western Front—we got our first taste of war; raw onions. That was all the food we ate on the trip, and that was only because we had managed to break into the supply car.

The next morning a brisk wind slapped us in face when we stepped off the platform, a sure sign winter was coming. The sky hung so low it looked like the inside of an airplane hanger. We headed to the airbase outside the city. Fifteen minutes later a beam of sunlight broke through the clouds, revealing a gleaming new B-24 Liberator waiting for us on the runway. Fresh off the Willow Run assembly line, the plane had everything—four 1,000 horse-power engines, compensating radio, gunnery sights, you name it.

Not only was the plane brand new, so was the crew. Except for Sandy, the captain, none of us had been battle-tested. We took the plane on a trial run—it flew like a charm—and we awaited our orders. When the orders came, off we went to the European Theatre.

Our flight plan called for leaving Lincoln at sundown. We were to refuel at Bangor, Maine, and then proceed across the Atlantic via Gander, Newfoundland, to the Azores Islands. From there it was on to Marrakesh, Morocco, across the Western Sahara to Algiers, and finally to our destination in southern Italy.

We didn't get very far before we ran into trouble. On the first leg of our flight, somewhere over Ohio in clouds as thick as pea soup, the wings of our brand new B-24 started to ice up.

"Can't you feel the drag?" someone said

The next thing we heard was Sandy's voice over the cockpit intercom: "Prepare to abandon flight."

We rushed to our stations and strapped on our parachutes. At two o'clock in the morning the exit bell rang and the bay doors opened. With Sandy still at the controls, the rest of us lined up ready to bail out. I was the first in line.

We waited for the bell to ring the second time—the signal to jump, just as we had been taught. We waited and waited, unaware that our adrenalin had made us impervious to the cold.

Eventually lights came into view on the ground and the bay doors closed. "All clear," Sandy's voice sounded on the intercom again. At five o'clock we landed in Bangor, just as our flight plan called for. When I asked Sandy how he got rid of the ice, he said with feigned nonchalance, "Easy, I dropped the plane five thousand feet."

The rest of the trip passed without incident. On the fifth day of February 1945 we landed at the 15th Air Force Base in Cerignola, Italy. Situated on the back side of the boot near the Adriatic coast, it was a town of little note except it boasted of green olives and a family named LaGuardia whose favorite son, a boy named Fiorello, grew up to become the mayor of New York City. The base itself was no more than a temporary airstrip for launching bombing raids against the Germans. A makeshift control tower jutted out from a cluster of whitewashed buildings. A half dozen barracks housed the enlisted men.

We had just settled into our bunks when the commanding officer, Colonel Snowden, called us into his office.

"Gentlemen," he said, pointing to a map. "I need you to fly up to northern Austria and take out an installation there. You'll probably encounter enemy fire."

My heart leapt to my throat. We all knew the trip would be a long one: three hundred miles up the Adriatic, then over the Alps and all the way up to northern Austria to hit our target and back again. Not only that, we'd be flying over German anti-aircraft guns once we passed the 45th parallel.

None of us spoke when we went back to our barracks. Without looking at each other we put on our fight jackets and headed out to the runway. We were about to board the plane when Billy Bruton said out of the blue, "Fellas, we gotta get down on our knees."

Hearing that from a GI, especially from Billy, surprised me. He had told me in one of our conversations back in Boise that he had been raised a Baptist, but we never talked religion beyond that. Now he was telling us to get down and pray.

His prayer must have worked, because we returned from our mission without so much as getting shot at. We picked up some food at the mess hall and collapsed into our bunks.

Now it was Tommy Lutz's turn to speak up: "Hey guys, we can't go to bed before we thank the Lord."

First it was Billy, now it was Tommy. I had grown up thinking if you weren't Christian Reformed your chances of getting to heaven were pretty slim. Billy had a shot at it because he was a Baptist. But Tommy was a Catholic, mind you, and weren't Catholics predestined for hell? I realized then and there that Tommy had as good a shot at getting to heaven as I did, maybe even a better one.

On another mission our assignment was to hit the Brenner Pass, the German army's main access route in the Alps between Austria and Italy. As we approached our target, I spotted anti-aircraft guns pointing up at us from the mountains.

We opened the bay doors and released a half-dozen 1,000-pound bombs, watching them explode when they hit the rocks. A few seconds later, through my headphones, I heard Troy Shields, our tail gunner, shout: "Anti-aircraft fire coming from behind!"

A clashing sound, like knives and forks dropping into my mom's enamel dishpan, hit the plane. Shrapnel. The plane jolted. The force of the explosion pushed the plane up and flattened me to the floor. I struggled back to my feet and heard Sandy's voice in my headphones: "Pete, you okay?"

One by one we checked in; it was standard procedure.

"Okay," I answered.

"Tommy?"

"Okay."

"Bill?"

"Okay."

"Troy?"

No answer.

THE WINGS OF WAR 53

"Troy?"

Still no answer.

My heart stopped. I scurried over to the turret and found Troy crumpled over, pale as a sheet but otherwise okay. The explosion's impact had disconnected his microphone.

So it went, more or less, for seven missions. Each time we hit our target, and each time we thanked God for bringing us back alive. But we knew we couldn't defy the odds forever. The law of averages would see to that.

⚜ ⚜ ⚜

May 7, 1945, early afternoon; A junior officer popped his head into the barracks and said, "Put on your dress uniforms. The colonel wants us to line up on the runway."

We had a hunch what was coming. After the Allies closed in from every direction—England from the north, the U.S. from the west and south, and the Russians from the east—the German forces were in a shambles.

We eagerly awaited confirmation of our hunch. After we assembled on the runway, Colonel Snowden's voice came over the P.A. "I suspect this comes as no surprise," he said, "but today the Germans announced their surrender."

When the cheering died down, the colonel continued: "Our chaplain will lead us in a prayer of thanksgiving."

When the chaplain finished his prayer, he handed the microphone back to the colonel.

"And now," the colonel said," we're going to celebrate!"

Two B-24s circled overhead.

"See those planes?" he asked, pointing to the sky. "This morning I ordered them up with a load of beer. When they come down, each man can have two bottles and no more. Is that clear?

Since the base lacked refrigerators, there was no way to chill the beer but to send it up on the planes. At ten thousand feet the beer was thirty degrees cooler than it would have been on the ground. When those planes came in, what a celebration we had! Who cared if it was two o'clock in the afternoon?

ᎧᏋᏟ ᎧᏋᏟ ᎧᏋᏟ

While most of the pilots were lieutenants, Sandy was a captain because of his combat experience. By the time of the German surrender he had become the colonel's personal assistant, and he took advantage of the perks. Rounding up the crew of his B-24 he said, "We're going on a little sightseeing trip."

Three hours later we were over Munich. He banked the plane low over the city so we could all get a good look. Seventy-one Allied air raids over a six-year period had reduced it to a pile of rubble.

But the war wasn't over. The Japanese were still going at it, and the 15th Air Force was getting ready to redeploy to the Pacific. I had packed my belongings and was all set to leave when an announcement came over the P.A. system: "VandenBosch report to headquarters immediately."

Colonel Snowden looked at me from behind a stack of papers on his desk. "You've been assigned to the Mediterranean Air Transport Command," he said. "An aircraft will be here tomorrow to pick you up."

My heart sank.

I returned to the barracks where my buddies were waiting—Troy, Bill, all the others. For six months I had been living with these guys, eating with them, flying with them. We were like brothers, and now I had to deliver this bombshell.

"I'm being redeployed," I said. "Mediterranean ATC. I'm leaving first thing tomorrow for Naples."

And just like that I was gone.

In Naples I learned terrestrial navigation and got hooked up to a new squadron. Our plane was a C-87, a transport version of the B-24. Every day we would fly generals, medical supplies, personnel and equipment to cities all over Europe and the Middle East—Berlin, Vienna, Athens, Cairo, Alexandria, Benghazi, you name it. In the space of two months I saw more of the world than I ever had before.

Then came another redeployment order. That was how the Air Corps worked: You got your notice, you packed, and off you went. No discussion. This time I was going to the Pacific on a supply ship.

I waited with my squadron at the deployment center while the ship was being loaded. With nothing else to do, my new buddy Ray Robinson and I went to see a concert the Andrews Sisters were putting on for the GIs. The auditorium was so full that guys were perched on rafters.

Despite the Andrews Sisters' attempt to lift our spirits, the mood was dour because most of us were being shipped out to the Pacific. One of the sisters, Patty, had just finished a number when the commanding officer came out on stage, tapped her on the shoulder, and whispered into her ear. Patty handed him the microphone.

The commanding officer held the microphone to his lips, drew in his breath, and said, "Japan has surrendered. The war is over."

You could have heard a pin drop.

"I repeat: the war is over," he said. "You don't have to go to the Pacific!"

At that instant pandemonium broke loose. Everyone in the auditorium hooted and hollered. Ray and I broke down and cried.

On the stage, Patty was crying too. "It's over! It's over!" she kept saying, apparently unaware that her microphone was still open.

A pair of GI fatigues dropped down from the rafters, followed by the guy who had worn them. He didn't care if he got hurt. Neither did the guys he landed on. They had been through a lot worse in combat, and now they were going home.

I hooted and hollered and cried with everybody else, because I was going home too.

Or so I thought.

Chapter Seven

Going Home

I had already missed going home once and wasn't very happy about it. My buddy Ray Robinson was in the same boat, so to speak. We decided since we weren't going home that we would grant ourselves a "leave." The Air Corps owed it to us, and by golly we deserved it.

Rome seemed the logical place to go; it was a two-hour drive up the coast from Naples, and I had never seen it on the ground, only from the air on my ATC flights. The only problem was, we had no way to get there.

Knowing full well we wouldn't get permission if we asked for it, we commandeered a motorcycle from an army depot and disguised it with a number from our outfit. On the back we tied two canvas sacks with our clothes inside and a cardboard box. Then off we sped on our joy-ride with me at the controls and Ray holding on for dear life.

So what was in the box? Enough cigarettes to kill a platoon. Thanks to the tobacco lobby in Washington, every GI was issued one pack of cigarettes a day. Companies like Philip Morris and R.J. Reynolds knew what they were doing: What better way to hook a soldier for life than to give him free cigarettes for two years? It was a smart investment.

Our plan after we got to Rome was to sell the cigarettes on the black market. Some of the cigarettes we had saved from our rations. Most of them we had collected from guys in our outfit, buying them at fifty-five cents a carton or writing their names down so we could pay them when we got back.

If you were to visit Rome today and needed a place to stay, your search might begin at the APT, the city's official tourist agency, and they would direct you to a hotel. But in 1945 the place to begin—at least for GIs on the town—was the Red Cross, which matched you up with a host family.

Our host family turned out to be a thirty-something-year old man and his wife and three children. They all spoke fluent English. When we arrived at their apartment, the man asked what we had in the box.

"Cigarettes," I said.

"Are you going to smoke them?"

"No, we're going to sell them." I didn't mention our plan to sell them on the black market; it was something people assumed.

"How much are you selling them for?"

"Twelve dollars a carton."

"How many cartons do you have?"

"Twenty. That's all we have in the box."

"I'll give you $200 for the box," he said.

"Sold," I said, and I collected his money.

Over the next five days the man and his wife showed us the sights of Rome—the Colosseum, the Roman Forum, Trevi Fountain, the Pantheon, the Vatican. They treated us like old friends. When it was time to leave, I felt guilty about charging him the $200 for the cigarettes and offered to refund his money.

"Oh no, you keep it," he said.

"But I took advantage…."

"No, no, no," he interrupted. "It's a small price to pay to have our freedom back. If you—the Americans—hadn't come, who knows what would have happened to us under Hitler?"

"Or Mussolini," his wife added.

Joe and I exchanged hugs with our Italian friends and waved from the motorcycle as we sped away. Two hours later we quietly returned the stolen motorcycle to its place at the army depot.

※ ※ ※

Now that the war was over, the Army Air Corps didn't seem to know what to do with me. Once again they deployed me to the ATC, this time to fly stretcher patients back to the United States. Mostly we flew C-46's, big old twin-engine props we called whales; that's how most of the wounded GIs got home. All the while I kept wondering when my turn would come to go home.

I had a lot of time to think on those flights. I befriended a guy on the plane named Gus Vandenberg. Among other things, we talked about religion. Gus was a Lutheran, and I became convinced he was going to heaven too, right along with Billy the Baptist and Tommy the Catholic. I came to realize you didn't have to be Christian Reformed to get to heaven.

In December my turn to go home finally came. While the plane loaded up on the tarmac, I lay in my bunk listening to Fred Waring and the Pennsylvanians. My mind drifted back to the choir room at Western Christian High School in Hull, Iowa, when my big brother John handed me his baton and said, "I want you to take over."

Now, waiting in Naples, Italy, for a plane to take me home, I imagined Fred Waring directing the Pennsylvanians with his baton –wasn't he doing the same thing I did as a high school kid? And I said to myself, "Of course he is, and I will do it again some day."

The plane was ready to take off. But at that moment a gust of wind off the Mediterranean blew another airplane into it, taking out the engine on the right wing. Once again I was stuck.

Thanks to a little intervention from the commanding officer (apparently he never found out about the motorcycle), my buddy Ray and I secured two places on the USS Monterey, an aircraft carrier bound for Newport News, Virginia.

We boarded the ship on the twenty-second of December. After the horn sounded, Ray and I stood on the deck and watched the dock slip away. I turned to him and said, "You know what's going to happen." It was a statement of fact more than a question.

"No, what's going to happen?" he asked.

"They're going to stop this ship at the Rock of Gilbraltar and they're going to announce over the P.A. system, 'Ray Robinson and Peter Vanden-Bosch come forward,' and they're going to take us off this ship and send us back."

Ray laughed. He obviously felt more confident about going home than

I did. It wasn't until we got twenty miles out into the Atlantic—out of sight of the Rock—that my jitters went away.

The voyage was rough, but I didn't care. On Christmas Day I stood on the deck and let the ocean spray hit my face.

As we proceeded across the Atlantic, the waves grew bigger. Even though the USS Monterey was longer than two football fields, it tossed back and forth like a teeter-totter. One night a stream of vomit rained down from the bunk above me and splattered on the floor.

Eventually the storm subsided. I craved a drink of milk. I hadn't had a drink of milk in two years, and it was something I had always taken for granted.

It occurred to me that freedom was something I had always taken for granted, too, just like drinking milk. If the war taught me anything, it was that freedom isn't handed to you like a glass of milk. You have to fight for it and die for it if necessary. My Italian friends didn't take their freedom for granted. I vowed never again to take my freedom for granted, either.

We arrived at Newport News on New Year's Eve, 1945. Ray and I watched from the deck of the USS Monterey as the first of the five thousand GIs onboard filed down the gangplank. A brass band waiting for us on shore struck up "America the Beautiful."

We made our way down to the gangplank and joined the procession. When Ray got off the ship he knelt down and kissed the ground.

When I got off the ship I knelt down and kissed the ground, too.

Chapter Eight

Finding a Path

At Newport News my buddy Ray and I boarded a military bus to Camp Atterbury, Indiana, for our discharge. The Air Corps offered to increase my rank two grades if I stayed in, from sergeant to tech sergeant. But after three years I'd had my fill of the military. I took my $120 discharge payment, packed my discharge papers in my canvas sack, and said goodbye to my buddy Ray.

When I arrived in Grand Rapids, I didn't want to go back to Bell Telephone and drop poles into the ground. So I counted up the money my wife had saved from my military pay plus the profits from my cigarette sales. We scraped together every nickel of our assets and bought a 1939 Ford Sedan. We packed our belongings in the car and set out for California like western pioneers. The only thing lacking was a "California or Bust" sign on the back bumper.

Edgerton, Minnesota, and Las Vegas, Nevada, may not have much in common, but they were important milestones in our trip. After our first day on the road we stopped in Edgerton to visit my parents. I hadn't seen them since taking off on that B-24 Liberator to southern Italy. What a moment that was, filled with emotion, my mother crying and praising God that I was home safely.

Several days later we wound our way down Route 66 into downtown Las Vegas—what people called "the strip." We stopped at a hotel on the strip—not something a Minnesota farm boy is accustomed to—and checked in for the night. The lobby was full of slot machines. The next morning when I paid the bill—everything was done in cash in those days—the desk clerk handed me a quarter in change. I slipped the quarter into a slot machine and pulled the lever. Jackpot! The payout was fifteen dollars. With gasoline at ten cents a gallon, my winnings covered the whole two thousand-mile trip from Grand Rapids, Michigan, to Bellflower, California—our destination.

Bellflower was a quiet southern California town of thirty thousand souls on the rural edge of Los Angeles County. Many of the inhabitants were second and third generation Dutch immigrants whose forebears had given up dairy farming in the old country in search of greener pastures. Holstein cows dotted the landscape before shopping centers, freeways and Disneyland took over.

One of the third generation Dutch émigrés in Bellflower was my older brother Tom, who discovered there was money to be made in the hay-hauling business.

"Just look at all those cattle," he said as I accompanied him on one of his deliveries. "You gotta get into the hay-hauling business, Pete. You'll make a fortune."

I took his advice and bought an International K7 semi-trailer truck. Every day while my wife waited at home I would drive out Highway 99 into the San Bernardino Valley or up to Bakersfield and load up the truck with bales. Then I'd strap them down and drive through the mountains back to Bellflower and drop them off and get home at two or three in the morning.

I was making good money, but after three months of this my wife—homesick and by herself most of the time—had had enough of being a hay-hauler's wife way out in California. She gave me an ultimatum; it was either her or the Holsteins. I had to choose, but she was going back to Michigan no matter what.

Choosing my wife over the Holsteins, I sold the truck, which broke my heart. Then back to Grand Rapids we went in our '39 Ford, my wife and I taking turns at the wheel.

So three months after moving to California, I was back in Grand Rapids looking for work. My hay-hauling experience, such as it was, helped me get a job driving a cement truck for the Grand Rapids Gravel Company. As before, I had to supply my own truck.

Dipping into the cash left over from selling the semi, I put $500 down with a dealer named Gingrich on a Diamond T cement-mixer truck. During my first days on the job my boss, Herman Meyers, a man old enough to be my father, rode with me in the cab and tried to instruct me in the fine points of the gravel business. But apparently I was more interested in discussing other things.

Finally, on the third day, Herman said, "Peter, I don't think you belong in this business. The way you talk, you belong in sales."

"But I got $500 down with Mr. Gingrich," I said.

"Well then, let's get it back."

Herman took me to Gingrich's office. "I'd like you to give this man his money back," he told the nonplussed truck dealer. "He's in the wrong business."

Gingrich refunded the $500. Although I didn't appreciate it as much then as I did later, Herman did me a huge favor.

But that still left me without a job. To make matters worse, millions of GIs back from the war were looking for work. In the *Grand Rapids Press* I saw an ad calling for a "tank-truck salesman" for Texaco Oil Company. "Ah," I thought, "I can drive truck. I can do sales with it." My only experience along that line had been in Italy selling those cigarettes on the black market. I chuckled to myself: "I'll just tell them I have international sales experience."

I talked my way into the job.

Every day I would drive down M-21 to the Texaco distribution center in Holland, fill up the tank-truck with gasoline, and deliver it to filling stations in Muskegon, Benton Harbor, Battle Creek, and Grand Rapids. "Trust your car to the man who wears the star," the jingo said. I was the man who wore the star.

But the job proved no more satisfying than eating Spam—and I'd had enough of that in the Air Corps. Late one afternoon, after completing my rounds and tucking the day's proceeds into my cash box, I was driving back to Holland on M-21. A car pulled beside my truck and I happened to look down. Behind the wheel sat a man in a three-piece suit, a briefcase on the seat beside him. "That's the kind of job I want," I thought. "If he can sell, I can sell."

When I got to the gas terminal I put the air brakes on, walked inside, and slapped the money on the counter. "I quit," I said, and I walked out.

More than I care to admit, I inherited some of my father's impulsiveness.

The next day I went to Bell Telephone, my old employer from before the war. Would they take me back? Not to install telephone poles, mind you, but to sell advertizing in the Yellow Pages. My brother Gerrit said they were looking for somebody to do that and I just might have an edge.

"Have you ever sold advertising?" the interviewer asked me.

"Cigarettes, yes. Hay, yes. Gasoline, yes. Advertising, no."

The interviewer smiled.

"But if I can sell *those* things, I can sell advertising," I said.

I got the job. Selling and relating to people one-on-one felt like the most natural thing I had ever done. I felt like my life—at least the working side of it—was moving in the right direction.

I was starting to realize some personal goals, too. After returning from California I had gone to a little airport at Comstock Park, a town outside Grand Rapids, run by two friends a few years out of high school, Rich DeVos and Jay VanAndel, who later went on to bigger things. I enrolled in the flight school at their airport. I had long given up on flying a P-38— there wasn't much need for P-38 pilots after the war anyway—but I figured I had a shot at owning my own airplane. For me that was a bigger thing than being a radio operator.

Twenty-five hours of flight time were required to qualify for the license exam. I passed it with flying colors—just as I had my radio operator's exam back in Sioux Falls—and two weeks later my FAA license arrived in the mail.

I kept on with flight school, first learning how to land on snow skis and then on pontoons. Aerobatics came next. An ex-Navy pilot, Harry Miller, taught me the maneuvers in a Fairchild PT-19. Before you knew it I was swooping the plane up to eight thousand feet, turning it upside down and letting it drop until it almost hit the ground and swooping it up again. I was making up for lost time. "No Ford Tri-Motor or B-24 could do this!" I told myself.

Through a flight club at the Kent County Airport, I bought into my first plane, a single-engine Cessna 182. It wasn't a Fairchild, but I had the satisfaction of being part owner of an airplane.

Finally I was doing what I had set out to do when I joined the Army Air Corps. Not that my time there had been wasted. A seed had been planted that was now bearing fruit. My childhood dream of flying was finally coming true. Now it was time to pursue my other dream: music.

I decided to organize a choral group, an all-male chorus of select voices that would specialize in Christian music. I would audition the singers myself, and the only way they would be accepted would be to pass my audition. I had no formal musical training, but neither did Lawrence Welk or Fred Waring, and if they could do it so could I.

Not quite knowing where to start, I went to see Trina Haan, the music director at Grand Rapids Christian High School. She had given lots of choir concerts in Grand Rapids, and everybody knew about her. I told her what my dream was, and she graciously gave me names of men who had sung at her school.

Then I went to see Professor Seymour Swets, the renowned choral director at Calvin College who had inspired me as a boy back in Edgerton. When I reminded him of our encounter at the church his eyes lit up. "Of course," he said, "you're the one who came up to me after the concert and said, 'How do I become a conductor?'"

"Yes!" I exclaimed, "and you said, 'Ask the Lord to lead you, and he will show you the way.'"

"And has he?"

"That's why I'm here!"

Professor Swets reached for a card file in his desk drawer and pulled out a handful of names. "Here, they're all alumni of mine," he said. "Why don't you audition them for your choral group?"

I recruited sixteen singers and came up with the name The King's Choraliers. Every Thursday night we gathered at the Back-to-God-Hour Chapel on Front Street and rehearsed our repertoire, each time adding a few new songs while fine-tuning others.

With sixteen choir robes lent to me by Professor Swets, we presented our first concert at the Twelfth Street Christian Reformed Church in the winter of 1951. The performance didn't draw a standing ovation, but my brother Gerrit came up to me afterwards and said, "I think Dad would be proud of you, Pete."

❦ ❦ ❦

Every so often I would go back to Edgerton to visit my parents. In 1955 my mother called and said, "Your father is sick. The doctor says he doesn't have long." She didn't specify what his illness was.

I hopped in my Cessna and a few hours later landed on an airstrip outside Edgerton. My sister Elizabeth met me there. When I walked in the front door, I dropped my bag on the floor and went upstairs to my parents' bedroom. My mother rose from her chair beside the bed and gave me a hug. "Thank you for coming, Peter. Your father is asleep."

I heard his voice from the bed. "Peter, you're here. Come." It was barely a whisper. He struggled to reach out his arms toward me.

I leaned over and kissed his forehead.

"Forgive me what I did," he said.

"Forgive you? For what?"

"For what I did that made you sleep in the cornfield."

I struggled to remember what he was talking about.

"You know, the time I threw the pitchfork at you."

I had long forgotten the incident, but it had weighed on my father's conscience for twenty years.

"Of course I forgive you, Dad," I said, somewhat bewildered.

Although the incident had happened so long ago, I felt the sensation of a weight being lifted from me as I spoke the words—a weight I had never been fully conscious of. My father must have felt that way too when he squeezed my hand. That was the last time I saw him. When he died a few weeks later I knew he was at peace and at home.

Chapter Nine

Music of the Angels

Life was good. I was flying, I was making music, my career was on track. What more could a guy want?

Despite all these positive things, all of that blue sky, two dark clouds lurked on the horizon. The first was a sense of incompleteness about all the success I was having, a kind of void that I couldn't put my finger on.

The second dark cloud was that my wife and I were unable to have children. But our prayers were answered in a sense when we were approved for adoption. Mary Joy was four months old when we picked her up at the Blodgett Home for Children the day before Christmas, 1956. Our son Mark was six weeks old when he joined our family in 1959.

The children were a blessing, but our marriage suffered. There was a growing distance between my wife and me, a gap that seemed to widen with each passing month.

Meanwhile, my career and musical life were humming along. Every Thursday night I would rehearse The King's Choraliers at the Back-to-God-Hour Chapel. A whole year passed before I felt we were ready for our next concert, but it was worth the wait. Wearing borrowed robes, we packed the Lee Street Christian Reformed Church.

After that performance The King's Choraliers took off. Our popularity grew with each concert. Before I knew it we had a waiting list: first tenors, second tenors, baritones, and basses. They were all lining up to get into the Choraliers. As I auditioned them we grew to twenty-four members.

In 1952 Bill Kuiper, who broadcast a weekly radio program in Grand

Rapids called "The Hour of Praise" on station WFUR, taped one of our early concerts. He played "O Worship the King," one of our songs, over and over on his program. We had taken the King's Choraliers name from the title and it had became our theme song.

A few years later, after the King's Choraliers had greatly improved, I stopped at his studio and asked if he would come out and record another concert.

Kuiper, a grey-haired man of around sixty, had an abrasive edge to him. "It's my station. I'll do with it as I please," was his gruff response.

I persisted. I had learned the importance of that if you wanted to achieve anything.

Eventually Kuiper warmed to the idea. "Okay, I'll record you again," he said.

I thanked him.

Kuiper wrinkled his brow, looked up at me from his desk, and said, "What do you do for a living?"

"I sell advertising for the Yellow Pages."

"How would you like to come work for me?"

"Excuse me?"

"I need a sales manager. You sold me on the King's Choraliers, so I know you can sell. What do you say?"

It was his turn to persuade me. Before I knew it I agreed, and I became the sales manager for WFUR, the flagship station for Furniture City Broadcasting. I worked hard at my new job and gradually advanced to sales manager for the company's three radio stations in Grand Rapids, Kalamazoo and Muskegon.

Kuiper called me into his office. "Peter, how would you like to be the general manager?"

"Would I *like* to?" I replied. "I would *love* to!"

"Hold on, it isn't quite time," he said. "The guy who has the job now doesn't know he's leaving. As soon as he does the job is yours."

"Is that a promise?"

"Yes, that's a promise."

Thanks to the work ethic drilled into me by my father, my promised promotion to general manager made me work all the harder. I wanted to make sure I deserved it when the time came.

Meanwhile, the King's Choraliers were putting on twenty concerts a year, mostly in churches on Sunday nights. Eventually invitations came from far and wide, even Canada. In the spring of 1958 we embarked on our first tour—to Iowa and South Dakota.

We started at Dordt College in Sioux Center, Iowa. After the concert a man I didn't recognize approached me on the chapel steps.

"Peter," he said, "I wonder if you could squeeze us into your tour?"

"Where?" I asked.

"The Christian Reformed Church in Edgerton, Minnesota."

My eyes popped. "That's my home church! Of course we'll do it!"

Just like that, we added Edgerton to our itinerary, seventy miles up the road from Sioux Center, Iowa. It was my first trip back since my father died.

During the concert I stood in the very spot where Professor Seymour Swets had stood twenty-three years before. I remembered the words he had spoken to me as a twelve-year-old: "Ask the Lord to lead you, and he will show you the way."

After we finished I turned to the congregation to acknowledge the standing ovation. I could see the pride in my mother's smile as she stood in the pew she had shared with my father. Now she was alone.

When the applause ended, the pastor invited the congregation to reassemble at the Christian school next door for a post-concert celebration. When I entered the room the applause started up again. Across the back wall stretched a banner that said, "Welcome Home, Peter!"

My mother was the first to come up and hug me. "I wish your father were here to see this," she said.

But amidst the celebration my mother sensed a kind of sadness in my mood, one of those dark clouds on my horizon. Mothers have a way of picking up on those things. When the last of the well-wishers left, I joined her at her table. She looked into my eyes and said, "Something is wrong, isn't it, Peter?"

I mumbled an acknowledgment.

"It's her, isn't it?" she said.

In my head I could still hear her response when I told her I was getting married: "Peter, are you sure you have the right one?"

"I just want you to be happy," she said, reaching for my hand across the table.

I should have listened to her, I thought. Now it was too late.

When she died the following year the Edgerton *Enterprise* proclaimed her a saint. But I had come to realize that she was also the wisest person I had ever known.

Chapter Ten

Finding Jesus at the Car Wash

When we returned from our tour, the Zondervan Corporation in Grand Rapids approached me about having The King's Choraliers record an album. Their request had an unusual codicil: Would we do it in Dutch?

Only a few of us in the chorus knew any Dutch, but since we couldn't resist the challenge we decided to do it. We recorded some Dutch Psalms and a Dutch version of "What a Friend We Have in Jesus."

Zondervan's enterprises included book publishing and radio broadcasting as well as making records. Apparently the powers-that-be were impressed enough with our Dutch album that they invited us to record one in English.

We made some 78s that sold quite well. Then we made an L.P. and named it after our theme song, "O Worship the King." That one sold well, too. Zondervan distributed our records not only in the United States but also in England, South Africa and Australia. We were good business for the company.

Meanwhile, at WFUR, Bill Kuiper announced that he had a new general manager. To my astonishment, it wasn't me; it was somebody else. To add insult to injury, it was somebody who in my opinion was less qualified for the job than I was.

When I heard the news I impulsively stormed into Kuiper's office and announced, "I quit!" (Once again, it wasn't just my father's work ethic that I inherited.)

He looked at me, startled. "You can't do that," he said.

"You bet I can! You made a promise, and you broke it!

Kuiper sat there with his mouth open.

"You *are not* to be trusted," I said, emphasizing the words *are not*. "I'm not working for somebody I can't trust. Good-bye."

That was that, and I left.

I felt a rush of exhilaration for having told him off, a kind of smugness one feels when expressing righteous indignation. But as soon as I left his office reality set it. Without a job, how was I going to support myself and my wife and two kids? By the time I pulled my car out of the parking lot, my righteous indignation had turned into panic.

Not knowing where to go or what to do, I did one of the most mundane things a person can do when he has just quit his job and doesn't have a clue where his next paycheck is coming from: I drove my car to the car wash.

I'm not a Catholic, but driving into one of those howling wind machines and having those monstrous brushes swoop down on you must be about the closest thing there is to Purgatory. And when you come out the other end and see daylight you feel cleansed and refreshed and ready to move on.

At least that's the way it's supposed to be. But I was just as distraught coming out of the car wash as I was going in. It must have shown on my face, because when I rolled my car window down I heard a voice say, "Hey buddy, what's wrong?" At first I thought I had imagined the voice, but when I turned to look out the window I saw a man motioning from the car beside me.

"Over here!" he said. "You look like you shouldn't be driving. Can I help you? Can I take you somewhere?"

Those were the kindest words I had ever heard from a stranger, but it was exactly what I needed to hear at that moment.

"Let's go get a cup of coffee," he said. "There's a restaurant across the street." I parked my car behind his and joined him in the restaurant.

"Name's Hal Sundberg," he said. He had the kindest face I had ever seen. "What's yours?"

"Pete VandenBosch," I said. I looked him closer in the face. "Say, haven't

I heard your name before? What do you do?"

"I'm the general manager of Channel 13, the new TV station here in town, if that means anything. And what do you do?"

"Well, until a half hour ago I was the sales manager for WFUR."

"No kidding. You say until a half hour ago?"

"Yeah, I just quit." I proceeded to spill out the whole story of the promise of my promotion and the betrayal by my boss.

"Well, I can see why you're upset," he said when I finished describing everything leading up to the car wash.

Sundberg paused for a moment and then resumed speaking. "Tell you what. I'm still putting together a staff. It so happens I'm looking for a sales manager. Would you care to apply?"

My mind flashed back to Major Miller, the army chaplain back in San Antonio, who asked me if I believed in providence. Whether it was providence or just plain luck that led me to Hal Sundberg, I didn't know. But as I looked at him across the table, I could have sworn I was looking at the face of Jesus. The strangest part was, I didn't know whether or not he was a Christian.

Providence or luck: Call it what you will. The following week I found myself behind the sales manager's desk at Channel 13. The first thing I needed was a sales staff, so I called several sales people I had hired and trained at WFUR. Would they like to join me at Channel 13? They did, and it didn't make Bill Kuiper very happy.

The next thing I knew, Channel 13, Hal Sundberg and I were named as co-defendants in a lawsuit filed by Kuiper.

"Don't worry about it," Sundberg said. "Our attorney will take care of it."

The court date came and I told my story to the judge. He threw the case out on the spot.

Apart from a nice salary increase and working for a boss I trusted, a fringe benefit of my new job was flying around the country to meet with advertising agencies. Instead of flying commercially and having to wait in long lines to check in—and this was before airport security—all I had to do was rent a plane from Northern Air, and off I went to cities like St. Louis and Cleveland and Milwaukee and Washington, D.C. I loved every minute of it.

One of my trips took me to Salt Lake City, Utah, where I attended a rehearsal of the Mormon Tabernacle Choir. As impressed as I was with this great choir, I thought, "I could do this in Grand Rapids!"

A few years later, in 1963, I started a second choral group, The Metropolitan Choir of Praise, comprised of mixed voices. By that time the King's Choraliers' reputation had become so widespread that one hundred and six people lined up outside the Bates Street Christian Reformed Church in Grand Rapids to audition for the choir.

Eventually I auditioned every singer (not all of them on the same day), and I told the ones who passed the audition, "Put your sheet music away. We're doing all of our concerts from memory."

So for the next ten years I directed both the King's Choraliers and the Metropolitan Choir.

Meanwhile, my career had taken a new twist. On November 23, 1963—the day after President Kennedy was shot—I received a phone call from Bernie Zondervan, the president of the Zondervan Corporation.

"Peter," he said, "we want to talk to you."

"About the King's Choraliers?"

"No, about a radio station we own, WJBL AM and FM in Holland - Ottawa Broadcasting. We want you to be the general manager. Can you come in and we'll talk about it?"

"Let me get back to you," I said.

The thought of leaving Channel 13 had never entered my head. I couldn't have been happier in my job, and Hal Sundberg was the kind of boss everyone dreamed of working for.

When Bernie Zondervan called the second time I reluctantly agreed to meet with him. He and his brother Pat and the company's accountant greeted me in the board room, and Bernie repeated his offer. "We want you to manage the station," he said. "After a year we'll give you the option to buy in."

"Look," I said, "I'm making $20,000 a year and I'm about to get a $7,800 raise. And I work for a terrific general manager who gives me free reign. Thank you, gentlemen, I appreciate your offer, but I'm going to turn it down. I hope this doesn't affect the King's Choraliers."

"Of course not," Bernie said, but I could hear the disappointment in his voice.

I thought that was the end of it, but three days later I got a letter from

Bernie with an offer beyond belief. I took the letter in to Hal Sundberg.

"Peter, this is one hell of an offer," he said. "You'll never get another one like it in your life."

"But I don't want to leave," I said. "I love it here."

"You should take this offer."

His response surprised me. This was the man who had rescued me at the car wash and given me a new lease on my career. This was the man who had restored my trust in human beings.

"You should take it," he repeated. "You'd be a fool to turn it down."

"What if I take my sales staff?" I was surprised to hear the words come out of my mouth.

"That's okay, we'll get other guys."

Hal Sundberg! What a different boss than the one I'd had before. But even with this assurance, I wasn't sure I could make the change. Bosses like Hal Sundberg came once in a lifetime, if you were lucky. That night I couldn't sleep a wink.

When I went back to Hal Sundberg the next morning, he was just as insistent as before: "Peter, you'll never get another offer like this. Take it."

And so in January 1964 I went to work at Ottawa Broadcasting and WJBL. I had a one-year option to buy forty-nine percent of the station at the same price Zondervan had paid five years before. I took the option and five years later bought the other one percent. As president and general manger I had complete control of the operation.

As WJBL grew I began to look at other radio stations. One, in Waukesha, Wisconsin, WAUK, caught my attention.

"Go ahead and buy it," was Zondervan's response.

"But I can't waste time driving around Lake Michigan to run it," I said.

"Then get an airplane," they said.

So I did—a twin-engine Comanche. It was in that plane that I made my first solo flight across Lake Michigan.

❧ ❧ ❧

June 1978. I was sitting at my desk at Ottawa Broadcasting when the phone rang. I picked it up. "VandenBosch," I said.

"Pete? Pete VandenBosch?" the voice said. It was familiar, but I could-
n't place it at first. "This is Bill Kuiper."

My heart skipped a beat. "What do you want?" I asked.

"I just want to talk to you for a minute," he said. There was a quality
in his voice, a kind of muted raspiness that I hadn't heard in the eight years
I had worked for him.

"Okay, I'm listening," I said. I put down my pen and pushed my chair
back from the desk.

"Pete, I have cancer." There was silence. And then he continued: "The
doctor said I have just a few weeks."

"I'm sorry to hear that," I said.

"I want you to know I'm deeply sorry for what happened," he said, his
voice choking. "My hands were tied. I had to give the general manager's job
to my son. I did what I had to do as a father. But I know it wasn't fair to you.
I broke my promise and I apologize."

I recognized another quality in his voice that I hadn't heard before: con-
trition.

"Bill, I forgive you," I said.

"Thank you, Pete," he said, after he composed himself.

"I want to thank you, too," I said.

"You want to thank *me*?"

"Yes, for giving me the opportunity to learn the broadcasting business,"
I said. "I wouldn't be here today if it hadn't been for you."

Even as I said, "Bill, I forgive you," I felt a burden being lifted, just as
I had felt when I forgave Heine Haitsma for bullying my sister and when I
forgave my father for throwing the pitchfork at me. How many lessons did
it take to learn the power of forgiveness?

As for Hal Sundberg, my boss at Channel 13, not once did we discuss
religion. He may have been an unbeliever for all I know. But to me he exem-
plified how a Christian life should be lived, because what I learned from
him was that all the platitudes and creeds in the world aren't worth a hill of
beans if you don't put the words into action.

Chapter Eleven

The Green Stick

The work ethic I inherited from my father served me well as long as it didn't interfere with my personal life. Then almost without realizing it, I let my working life take over. By 1973 I was running four radio stations and a billboard company. If I wasn't flying to St. Louis or Milwaukee to close a business deal I was rehearsing the King's Choraliers or the Metropolitan Choir for our next performance or concert tour. It seemed like work filled every minute of every day of my week.

And I was married with two teenage children.

Despite how busy I was, I felt a gnawing sense of emptiness in my life. Around that time an autobiography by the English writer Malcolm Muggeridge came out called *Chronicles of Wasted Time.* In that book he talked about the Russian novelist Leo Tolstoy and the emptiness he felt in spite of his huge success with *War and Peace.*

"There I was," Tolstoy said of himself, "a man in my fifties. I was successful as a writer beyond the wildest dreams I had ever entertained. I was famous. I was rich. I had every single gift that a human being could possibly want. And yet I had to hide away a rope that was hanging in my study for fear that I would destroy myself."

Why did Tolstoy feel like that? It was because, in spite of his material success and acclaim, he found no real purpose in his life.

Tolstoy imagined that somewhere on his estate near Moscow was buried a green stick, and on that stick was carved the secret of everlasting happiness, and if he could find that stick he would discover the answer to the question,

"Why did God put me here?" Over time, a legend grew up about his quest for the Green Stick.

If God had a plan for my life, he hadn't bothered to tell me. Or else I wasn't listening. Maybe a green stick was waiting for *me* somewhere to discover its secret, but I wasn't looking. I just kept racing from one busy day to the next.

Despite the emptiness I felt in my life, it was pretty much business as usual. A few years after we bought WAUK, the radio station in Waukesha, I turned it into the black. I managed to do the same with a billboard company, and I owned stock in the Zondervan Corporation.

After Bernie Zondervan died in 1966, his brother Pat took over the company. With a new captain at the helm the ship was changing course.

Pat called me into his office.

"You're doing so well with the radio stations," he said. "How would you like to run Singcord and Singspiration, too?" Singcord was Zondervan's record label and Singspiration its sheet music division.

"I don't want to do that," I replied.

"What *do* you want to do?" Pat asked.

"I don't know."

"Would you care to buy out Ottawa Broadcasting?"

"Why? Is Zondervan getting out of the broadcasting business?"

"Yes."

So in 1973 Zondervan sold the station in Waukesha and I bought out Ottawa Broadcasting, which included WJBL AM and FM. We had sold off the billboard company which simplified my life somewhat, but I was still working too hard to pay attention to any higher calling God had in store for me.

That led to one of the most difficult decisions of my life: to give up the King's Choraliers.

The Choraliers had been a huge part of my life since 1950. Five jobs had come and four had gone in that time, but the Choraliers were a constant. Although I had never been paid for directing them, the Choraliers had given me some wonderful gifts over the years including a 30.6 calibre Belgian hunting rifle. The inscription on it reads: "Presented to Peter J. VandenBosch, our director and founder, for his dedicated leadership."

I directed the King's Choraliers for the last time in September 1973. When we finished the last number, "Saviour, Like a Shepherd Lead Us," I had tears in my eyes. During my twenty-three years with them we had recorded ten albums that aired on four continents, and we had toured all over the country in venues as humble as my home church in Edgerton, Minnesota, and as spectacular as the United States Air Force Academy in Colorado Springs, Colorado.

The King's Choraliers didn't stop when I retired. They're still going strong today. But when I gave them up in 1973, and then the Metropolitan Choir in 1977, I still didn't find the happiness I was looking for. I was still looking for the Green Stick.

Chapter Twelve

A Still, Small Voice

My wife and I divorced in 1978. At the time I was a member of Providence Christian Reformed Church in Grand Rapids. The junior choir director there was a woman named Joan Marie Marcus. She had also had a difficult marriage which ended in divorce. At first we were just friends. Then we started seeing each other, and it was like magic. Since we knew from experience what made a bad marriage, we also knew what it would take to make a good marriage. We decided to give it a try. When I proposed to her she accepted, and we got married on September 29, 1978.

I haven't regretted it for a minute.

In 1983 I took stock of my situation. On the home front I was happily married. On the business front my investment in the broadcasting business had multiplied fifty-two times. I knew if I managed my finances carefully I could retire in leisure. With my musical and professional life behind me, I decided I had done enough in the way of public service.

I was living the dream. I had a house in Florida and a house in Michigan, a car at either end, and I would fly my own airplane back and forth between the two. I had a boat for fishing on Lake Michigan and one for fishing on the Gulf of Mexico.

"This is what people aspire to," I told myself. And I had done it by the age of sixty. I had retired early and in good health.

Joan and I continued to travel. We started exploring the islands of the Caribbean. Sometimes we would fly down and stay in a classy hotel.

Sometimes we would board a cruise ship and ride the waves.

In the back of my mind, though, there was always a shadow, a vague sense of incompleteness. Whenever thoughts like that came to the surface I would try to ignore them or dispel them with a trip to the Bahamas or Key West or some Caribbean island we hadn't yet explored.

Invariably, though, our lives would fall back into the same pattern after we returned from one of our jaunts. Joan and I would get up in the morning and first figure out what to wear: the white shirt or the blue one?

Then I would figure out what to do: Go fishing? Play golf? Play bocce ball? Where? With whom?

Joan would figure out where to go shopping: the Waterside Shops? Fifth Avenue South? Then she would figure out what to buy: a new pair of shoes? Something for the living room? If so, which house? Florida or Michigan?

In the evening our biggest problem was figuring out where to eat: the Bonefish Grill? The Mangrove Cafe? Did I want steak or seafood? Maybe the Surf 'n Turf?

We were living the American dream in our retirement, surrounded mainly by other retired people trying to figure out the same things. More and more, I wondered what it was we had figured out. There were so many talented people, yet they were doing nothing more meaningful with their lives than we were.

"So this is what people aspire to," I kept telling myself. "How many people would like to be in my shoes?" Then I wondered if I wanted to be in my own shoes. I started to pose it as a question: "Is this what people really aspire to?"

One positive thing was the fishing. I liked getting out on the boat and feeling the gentle rocking motion of the waves. I liked the blue sky and water.

Out at sea you can sit for hours staring at a line stretching out into the blue expanse and think your own thoughts. Sometimes you imagine a big fish at the other end of the line and you play out the battle in your head, every tug and bend of the rod. Sometimes you think about the people in your life: your wife, children and grandchildren. Sometimes you think about nothing in particular.

On that day in November, the nothing in particular I was thinking about was how many grouper we were going to catch. Joe was a good fish tracker, one of the best, so expectations in the boat were high that day. I turned to look at him. Gazing out from starboard, he apparently was lost in thoughts of his own or looking for grouper. Up in the bow sat Indie. It occurred to me that I didn't know his real name. All I knew was he came from Indiana.

Across from Indie up in the bow sat Al Zimmerman, one of my oldest friends. How many New Year's Eves had we spent together? Ten? Fifteen? Al, who had been with me through good times and bad.

I turned to the water again. It had a smooth, glass-like quality to it. My thoughts returned to the grouper. Yes, we'll have a good haul today.

That's when I heard the voice. "Peter," it said.

I turned around and looked at Al and Indie and Joe. All three were gazing out over the water; it was obvious none of them had said anything. I turned back and checked my line.

"Peter."

I looked at my buddies again. Nothing, no sign that any of them had said—or heard—anything.

"Peter," the voice said again. This time it was more distinct—soft and gentle yet more distinct. "*Peter,*" it said, "*there is more to life than this.*"

Once more the voice spoke. This time it was more like an echo: "Peter, there is more to life than this."

My hands shook. Blood ran from my head, my knees grew weak. I tried to keep from fainting. To my fishing buddies I said nothing. To Joan, when I got home late that afternoon, I said nothing. The voice echoed inside of me for two weeks. I turned inward, contemplating what had happened, not knowing what to make of it or what to do.

ఆ ఆ ఆ

Joan noticed the change that had come over me, and I knew I couldn't keep it from her forever. Finally I worked up the nerve to tell her.

We went out for a picnic in an orange grove by the Caloosahatchee River. When we arrived we spread the table cloth out on a picnic table and unpacked the basket. We sat down.

"Joan," I said, "there's something I have to tell you."

I could see in her face that she knew this was going to be important. I was still frightened of how she would react.

"Two weeks ago, out on the boat, something happened."

"What happened, Honey?"

"I heard a voice." I turned away, struggling to maintain my composure. "I heard a voice," I said again. I took a deep breath and looked Joan directly in the eye. "It was the voice of God, Joan. God spoke to me."

Joan held my gaze. "What did he say?"

"He said, 'Peter, there is more to life than this.' And that was it."

"That was it?"

"That was it."

But as I was about to discover, God seldom reveals himself in one eureka moment. More often he does it subtly and step-by-step.

When I heard God's voice on the boat, it was merely to get my attention. By the time I got the drift of what he was telling me, God would have to speak to me three more times. And each time he would speak to me through someone else's voice.

So now the question was, Whose voice would God use next? And what would the voice tell me?

It didn't take me long to find out. And what the voice told me would change my life.

Chapter Thirteen

Going Home Again

The second time God spoke to me was through Joan's voice. "Honey," she said, "We have to sell the house here and go home to Michigan."

I was relieved and dumbfounded: relieved because Joan had taken my revelation seriously, dumbfounded because her response wasn't the one I had expected to hear, not in a million years.

Most of all I was scared, because God was finally revealing his plan to me, and it wasn't the plan I had for myself.

I looked at Joan. "You're kidding, right?" I said. "Sell our beautiful house here in Florida? You're not serious!"

"I'm dead serious," she said. The tone in her voice left no doubt.

By February we had put our Florida house up for sale, got rid of the boat, and moved back to Michigan.

If a car wash tunnel is the closest thing to Purgatory, February in Michigan is the next closest thing. The Lake Michigan shoreline is a mass of ice jams, and bitter wind pierces through the buttons of your coat, chilling you to the core. Moving back to Michigan wasn't my idea of a fairy tale ("and they lived happily ever after"), not by a long shot.

Indeed, most of our friends thought we had lost our minds. "What are you doing here?" they would ask. "Is something wrong with your marriage?" "Is your health all right?" "Do you have financial problems?" All of their questions boiled down to "Why in the world did you come back?"

I didn't know the answer. All I knew was that we had to be back in Michigan. I was still waiting to find out why.

But I had to say something. I had several stock responses, such as "We just got tired of taking care of so much stuff," or "We were getting bored on the cruise ships and the food in the exclusive clubs all tastes the same." Their cocked eyebrows told me they weren't convinced.

Every time I answered them, the voice on the boat would come back to me: "Peter, there is more to life than this."

Some things made it easier to come back, like our grandchildren. Whenever Joan and I left for Florida we would kiss them goodbye and tell them how much we would miss them.

On one of those good-byes little Deanna, with all the clarity of a three-year-old, said, "Well, if you miss us so much, then how come you go to Florida?" We knew we wouldn't have to answer her question anymore.

Still, the question came from our friends: "Why did you come back?"

I started giving an answer that came a bit closer to the truth: "Retirement isn't so great when you don't have anything to do with your time."

Boy, did people jump on that. Colleagues and would-be business partners started coming out of the woodwork. I had one offer to invest in a radio station and sit on the board. I had another offer to buy into a furniture business.

I turned each offer down, because the voice from the boat kept coming back to me. I knew I had to do something meaningful with my life. But what?

People kept prodding me, and my excuses kept falling short.

Joan was as patient as an angel. Not once did she pressure me into making a decision or to take one of those offers.

I just waited for God to reveal his plan to me. February turned into March. March turned into April. Still I waited. And I prayed.

As the April showers gave way to the May flowers, I was getting restless. I got that burst of energy that springtime always brings, but I didn't know what to do with it. It was months ago that God had spoken to me. Then nothing. How was I supposed to know what his plan was for me?

I prayed for an answer. "God," I said, "if you want me to do something with my life you have to make it real plain. I'm listening, but I'm not sure what I'm listening for. What is the 'more than this' you want me to find?"

Before the month was out my prayer was answered. The third time God spoke to me was through the voice of an old friend, and it was by telephone.

"Hey, Peter," came his booming voice, "it's Les Slagh." I had once owned a plane with Les, and we had kept a close friendship through the years.

"Hi Les, it's been a while. How are you doing?"

He got right to the point. "Peter, why don't you use your plane to fly low income people in need of medical treatment to their appointments and do it for free?"

I thanked Les for the idea and hung up. The phone call lasted all of thirty seconds.

I sat staring into space for a minute. Then I rose from the chair and went downstairs.

Joan was sitting at the kitchen table.

"Honey," I said, "Les Slagh just called me on the phone."

Joan stopped what she was doing and looked up. "So what did you two talk about?"

"He says I should fly low-income patients around the country for medical treatment and do it for free."

Now I had prayed to God to make it real plain to me what his plan was, and that's exactly what he did. The fourth time God spoke to me it was through Joan's voice, and he was making his message as plain as could be.

Joan pointed at me and said, "There's your call!"

Of course! Yes! It all made sense. That was my call. Everything in my life had been preparing me for it. The tri-plane flying over the fields in Edgerton inspired in me a passion for flying. My time as radio operator in the war reinforced my love of flying and prepared me for the broadcasting business. My business and musical careers helped me develop the management skills I would need to start up and run a nonprofit organization. Of course, it all came together!

A few more weeks went by before I realized that God was done speaking to me. He had given me all the direction I needed. Now it was up to me to get off my butt and act.

And so in June of 1991 I got into my car and drove to Holland Hospital. I parked, walked in through the main entrance, and to the Office of Social Services.

The receptionist looked up from her computer. "Can I help you?" she asked.

"Actually," I replied, "I was wondering the same thing."

Chapter Fourteen

Taking Flight

The ninth day of July, 1991, dawned sunny and dry. The temperature was seventy-five degrees and there wasn't a cloud in the sky. A light breeze blew across the Tulip City Airport in Holland as I did the routine pre-flight checks in my twin engine, six-passenger Seneca II. Next to me was Carleton Wright, Jr. who would serve as my co-pilot.

Holland Hospital had called me a few days before to take me up on my offer. Two children, a brother and sister, needed specialized treatment at the Mayo Clinic in Rochester, Minnesota. Their mother would fly out there with us.

I had arranged the flight and called Carl, a pilot based in Muskegon, Michigan, to ask if he would fly with me. Carl had thousands of flight hours and I wanted someone with experience for the job. This was to be the first flight for an organization that began with God's voice on the boat. My wife, Joan, had come up with the name: Wings of Mercy.

A car drove up and our passengers got out. Lulu Lara was sixteen years old and her brother Hector was nineteen. They both suffered from a condition known as Rothmund-Thomson Syndrome, an early aging disease compounded by cancer.

Lulu was about three feet tall, Hector about three-feet-six. Their mother, Bianca, got out of the car and struggled to take their bags from the trunk.

I hopped out of the plane and walked over. "Hi, I'm Mr. VandenBosch. Nice to meet you. Let me help you with that." I picked up the bags.

"Do you like airplanes?" I asked the kids.

"We've never been in one," Lulu answered.

"This one looks so small," Hector added. I could tell they were nervous.

"Don't be scared," I said. "I've done this lots of times on days lots worse than this. You couldn't ask for a better day." I smiled as I loaded their bags into the plane.

I helped the children in and was about to offer my hand to help the mother. She paused.

"I want to thank you," she said. "But I don't have the words. I don't know how to thank you enough."

I could tell she was trying to hold back tears. She stepped forward and hugged me. I had to fight back tears of my own.

In the plane, I shut the door and reminded them to buckle their seat belts. I put on my headset and did the final checks.

"All right, we're ready," I said. "Are you?"

"Yes," they replied in a chorus.

I fired the engines and the propellers roared to life. We taxied toward the runway.

"Here we go," I said. I turned around and smiled at them.

The plane gathered speed on the runway. The wind rushed by. We went faster and faster. The air pushed under the wings, and pulled from above. The wheels lifted off the runway. I pointed the nose towards the heavens and we ascended.

That was the day I found the Green Stick.

PART TWO

The First 20 Years

Wings of Mercy had its spiritual beginning in November 1990 when I heard God's voice in the fishing boat off the Florida coast. After the fateful phone call from Les Slagh proposing that I fly patients for free to distant medical facilities, the organization took shape. My wife Joan prepared the following chronology highlighting Wings of Mercy's first twenty years.

1991

JUNE. The first organizational meeting of Wings of Mercy is held June 24 at the Best Western Hotel in Holland. The meeting draws a number of local pilots thanks to a front-page article in the *Holland Sentinel*.

JULY. Wings of Mercy flies its first mission on July 9. Peter Vanden-Bosch and co-pilot Carleton Wright, Jr. fly Bianca Lara's children Hector and Lulu from Holland, Michigan, to Rochester, Minnesota, for treatment at the Mayo Clinic.

JULY. The Articles of Incorporation are filed with the State of Michigan, and the first Board of Directors is elected. The first board members are Peter VandenBosch, president and treasurer; Lee Helmink, vice president; Rick Siegers, secretary; Joel Spykerman and Carleton Wright, Jr.

JULY. Jay VanDaalen and Russ Hyma are the first aircraft owners to join Wings of Mercy's team of pilots.

AUGUST. Wings of Mercy, Inc. is officially registered as a 501(c)(3) non-profit organization. The VFW presents Peter VandenBosch and Rick Siegers with a $25 check, Wings of Mercy's first contribution.

1992

MAY. The Wings of Mercy logo is registered as a U.S. trademark.

JUNE. The first Holland fly-in breakfast is held at Tulip City Airport on Peter's 69th birthday, June 12. About 50 people attend the event catered by Donna Dreyer, a Wings volunteer. The State of Michigan honors Peter for founding the organization.

SEPTEMBER. A Wings of Mercy membership meeting is held at the Mason County Airport in Ludington, Michigan—the organization's first outreach beyond Holland. Among those present are Carol and Jerry Hause of Lansing whose son Jerry Jr., a Wings pilot, was killed two months before in an unrelated accident. The Hauses later sponsor a Wings fundraiser in Lansing—a marathon in their son's honor.

1993

DECEMBER. The first Wings of Mercy newsletter is published. Edited by John Workman, the first issue contains a list of flights and pilots, letters from grateful patients and families, and an announcement that the Prince Corporation has included Wings of Mercy in its annual matching gift program. The holiday tradition continued for 17 years through Prince's successor corporation, Johnson Controls, Inc. (JCI).

1994

APRIL. The newly-renamed *Wings Flyer* is published. A month later, Sharon Scanlon is named editor. Today, *Wings Flyer* is printed every spring and fall in an attractive, professional format and sent to contributors, volunteers and pilots.

APRIL. Bud Godmair is named Wings of Mercy's first flight director. A year later a woman patient whose flight he has arranged to the Mayo Clinic proposes to him and he accepts. Bud and Mary Godmair are married August 29, 1995.

OCTOBER. Hope College produces a free fundraising video for Wings of Mercy. Meanwhile, Wings expands its service to northern lower Michigan. Flights out of Traverse City are added to those out Holland, Grand Rapids, South Haven, Muskegon, Battle Creek, Fremont, Kalamazoo, Lansing and Three Rivers.

1995

FEBRUARY. Dr. David Van Nostrand, a surgeon from St. Cloud, Minnesota, starts the first Wings of Mercy chapter outside Michigan: Wings of Mercy Minnesota.

APRIL. The Board of Directors approves new operational guidelines. Wings of Mercy Minnesota's inaugural flight takes place April 7.

JULY. Peter VandenBosch and co-pilot Les Reminga fly what is now Wings of Mercy West Michigan's 500th mission on July 9. The flight takes place on the fourth anniversary of the first mission.

OCTOBER. The 500th mission is celebrated with a dinner and fundraising auction at the Holiday Inn in Holland.

1996

MARCH. Cody Welsh, an east Michigan-based Northwest Airlines pilot, starts the third Wings of Mercy chapter: Wings of Mercy East Michigan.

JUNE. More than 500 people attend Wings of Mercy West Michigan's first annual fly-in and pancake breakfast at Muskegon County Airport. Breakfast is served by the Muskegon Lions Club.

AUGUST. Charter board member Rick Siegers steps down with this benchmark for Wings of Mercy: "Keep this organization squeaky clean, and never be ashamed of the name of Jesus Christ."

1997

MAY. Attendance at the second annual Muskegon-based Wings of Mercy West Michigan fly-in and pancake breakfast grows to 680. The Muskegon Lions Club again serves breakfast. "Wings Wear" clothing is introduced with the Wings of Mercy logo.

JULY. The purchase of a $7,000 FAA-certified stretcher is made possible with contributions from the Muskegon Community Foundation and the Rotary Foundation.

1998

JUNE. Reorganization of the flight director position results in the Good Samaritan Center of Holland screening patients calls. Jenn Fettig, a social service specialist, assumes screening duties while Bud Godmair continues as chief flight coordinator.

AUGUST. Russ Hyma and Jay VanDaalen fly Wings of Mercy West Michigan's 1000th patient, Andrea Kelly, to Boston's St. Elizabeth Hospital on August 30.

NOVEMBER. Wings of Mercy West Michigan celebrates its 1000th mission with a fundraising banquet at Sandy Point Restaurant in Holland. The featured speaker is former NASA astronaut Col. Jack Lousma who shows videos of the historic Apollo-Soyuz space station docking and the third Columbia shuttle mission which he commanded in March 1982.

1999

JANUARY. Carla Lokers becomes Wings of Mercy West Michigan's first full-time employee as flight director/patient screener, effectively combining both responsibilities.

JUNE. Wings of Mercy's first "CareAffaire" fly-in fundraiser, is held at Holland's Tulip City Airport. All subsequent fly-ins carry the name "CareAffaire," followed by the name of the host city.

2000

JULY. Wings of Mercy West Michigan expands its Michigan residency requirement to Illinois, Indiana, Ohio and Wisconsin.

2001

FEBRUARY. Ron Cathey succeeds Carla Lokers as flight director.

JULY. Wings of Mercy celebrates its 10th anniversary with two CareAffaire fundraisers in Holland and Muskegon. Total miles traveled since July 9, 2001: 1,357,290. Total patients served: 1,500.

SEPTEMBER. Wings of Mercy flies patient Water Johnson to the Cleveland Clinic on September 12, the day after the World Trade Center attack. The flight tests Wings of Mercy's "lifeguard priority" in the sky under high security conditions. (See Walter's first-hand account in Part Three.)

2002

FEBRUARY. Wings of Mercy West Michigan flies its 1500th mission on February 16. The event is celebrated at a "Flight 1500" benefit dinner at the Watermark County Club in Grand Rapids.

MAY. Wings of Mercy Illiana is welcomed into the Wings of Mercy organization with Jim Butler as president.

SEPTEMBER. Rob Becker's Cedar Crest Dairy hosts the first of three annual ice cream socials to benefit Wings of Mercy.

DECEMBER. Sharon Huminsky, part-time flight coordinator since September, assumes the responsibility full-time.

2003

July. The first annual Wings of Mercy pig roast benefit is held at Plane View Banquet Center. In 2010 the venue changes to the Holland Fish and Game Club.

2004

June. Wings of Mercy West Michigan flies its 2000th mission June 16 out of Gerald R. Ford International Airport in Grand Rapids. The pilots are Bud Post and Harold Goehring. Wings of Mercy Illiana ceases operations.

September. The first CareAffaire Grand Rapids is held on the third anniversary of the 9/11 attack. A moment of silence is observed at 9 o'clock.

September. The 2000th mission is celebrated a week later at a dinner hosted by Jim and Ginger Juries at the Holland Country Club. The ostensible purpose is to honor the pilots. Instead, Peter VandenBosch is surprised to find out that he is the honoree. A color guard presents him with an American flag. Holland mayor Al McGeehan gives him a key to the city. And patient Sonnie Bryant moves the audience with her description of what Wings of Mercy did for her. (See her testimonial in Part Three.)

2005

June. CareAffaire Holland holds a South Washington Avenue tunnel walk under a new runway at Tulip City Airport. Priority Health, the sponsor, matches all funds raised at the tunnel walk.

September. Wings of Mercy pilots Dan Horne and Harold Goerhing partner with Michigan-based International Aid to fly volunteers and supplies to New Orleans after Hurricane Katrina.

2006

May. Gary VanderVeen and Dan Horne fly the 2,500th Wings of Mercy West Michigan mission May 17, returning Jill DeVries from Florida to Holland's Tulip City Airport.

JUNE. Wings of Mercy celebrates its 15th anniversary at three separate events: CareAffaire Muskegon, CareAffaire Grand Rapids, and CareAffaire Holland Mike Workman organizes the first Run for Wings marathon at the Muskegon event.

2007

AUGUST. Sharon Huminsky assumes flight coordinator position. Wings of Mercy West Michigan moves to new quarters in Zeeland, Michigan.

SEPTEMBER. The first CareAffaire Traverse City event is held at Cherry Capital Airport, spearheaded by Mark Evans.

SEPTEMBER. The National Aeronautic Association and Air Care Alliance honor Peter VandenBosch with the 2007 Public Benefit Flying Award. Presented September 17 at the U.S. Capitol in Washington, D.C., the award cites Peter "for being the wind beneath the wings for Wings of Mercy thereby easing the lives of countless persons."

2008

OCTOBER. The leadership torch is passed from Peter VandenBosch to Terry Boer, who succeeds Peter as Wings of Mercy president. The event takes place at an October 10 fundraiser at the Pinnacle in Hudsonville, Michigan. The program features U.S. Congressman Pete Hoekstra as the guest speaker and The King's Choraliers in a surprise performance. Dan Horne is named vice president and operations director.

2009

JULY. Wings of Mercy participates in the Experimental Aircraft Air-Venture in Oshkosh, Wisconsin, marking its entrance on the national stage. Peter VandenBosch is one of four participants in a Fly-for-Life roundtable hosted by former CNN science editor Miles O'Brien.

2010

JANUARY. Grace Spelde joins the Wings of Mercy West Michigan staff as Flight Coordinator and Sharon Huminsky as Flight Director.

MAY. Wings of Mercy West Michigan moves to its new location at City on the Hill in Zeeland, Michigan.

AUGUST. Seven hundred fifty people—a sell-out crowd—descend on House of Chan in Muskegon, Michigan, for a Wings of Mercy fish fry hosted by Joe Chan, John Workman, and the Doo Drop Inn staff.

NOVEMBER. Peter VandenBosch begins organizing a Wings of Mercy West Michigan fundraising staff to serve Holland, Grand Rapids, Muskegon and Traverse City.

Wings of Mercy continues to grow. At this writing the West Michigan chapter alone flies an average of 27 missions a month. Special thanks are due to Terry Boer and Dan Horne who have worked tirelessly with the FAA on behalf of Wings, and the 300 volunteer pilots who have made a difference in people's lives.

—COMPILED BY JOAN VANDENBOSCH

PART THREE

'Dear Earth Angels'

Since its founding in 1991, Wings of Mercy has flown thousands of life-saving medical missions to such places as the Mayo Clinic in Rochester, Minnesota, and John Hopkins University Hospital in Baltimore, Maryland. Five of the patients who have benefitted from these missions and the mother of another describe how Wings of Mercy helped them through their crises:

Sonnie Bryant

Several years ago I was diagnosed with a disease called transitional cell carcinoma, an aggressive cancer that attacks the kidneys and bladder. I didn't fit the profile of someone afflicted with this disease. According to the profile, I should have been a seventy-five-year-old cigar-smoking man, not a thirty-something-year-old woman who always took care of herself.

Before I became ill I had my own clothes-design business, but the travel and stress proved too much for me. To complicate matters, my husband and I were getting a divorce. So besides being sick and unable to run my own business I was without health insurance.

In order to have health insurance I found a desk job. When my employer found out about my condition he let me go. Then I interviewed with another employer, Siegers Seed Company, and was hired as a personnel assistant.

One morning when I was getting ready for work I turned on the radio, which I never do before work. Peter VandenBosch was being interviewed about Wings of Mercy and the free service they provide for people who need specialized medical care.

On my lunch break I called the number he gave on the air. What followed were dozens of flights to the Mayo Clinic in Rochester, Minnesota, for surgery and check-ups and other procedures I would need every two or three months.

Coincidentally, one day at work Rick Siegers, the company president, asked me, "Are you familiar with Wings of Mercy?"

"Yes, I am," I said.

"Well, I'm a Wings of Mercy pilot, and I saw in the flight records a patient whose name is the same as yours."

"That's me!" I said.

Rick flew me to Mayo himself after that. What a boss!

But that's not the end of my story. One evening I met Marcel Easter at a dinner party. I wasn't looking to meet anyone, but something just clicked between us. I called my mother and said, "Mom, I'm losing my hair and I met this really great guy." He didn't care about my hair. He cared about me.

Marcel, who runs a construction company, has a seventh degree black belt in taekwondo. He is always there for me. He holds my head when I throw up. He'll even crawl into a bathroom stall at a restaurant to see if I am all right. Yes, he actually did that once.

Marcel has helped me live with myself. When I hesitated to show him one of my surgical scars, he said, "Don't be ashamed. It's beautiful. It shows that you're here and you're alive."

Marcel is an angel.

So are Peter VandenBosch and Rick Siegers and all the other people connected with Wings of Mercy. If it weren't for them I wouldn't be alive today to show Marcel my scar.

Walter Johnson

I had always been the athletic type. In high school I played basketball and baseball and ran track. At Oakland University I played basketball. Later I played basketball with a semi-pro team affiliated with the Harlem Globe-trotters.

But all that ended when my back went out in 1988. I was delivering a package when it happened. The doctor told me I had a spinal injury and would need multiple surgeries. He told me I would never play ball again.

My fifth back surgery was scheduled at the Cleveland Clinic. I drove there in my car and realized after the surgery there was no way I could drive back to Michigan. The hospital put me in touch with Wings of Mercy for the trip home.

Bob Van Strien flew to Cleveland to pick me up. It was the first time I had ever hugged a white man.

It was also the first time I had flown in a small plane. I felt every wind

pocket, every pump of turbulence. Each time the plane bounced a shooting pain went up my spine. After I got home, Bob called to see if I was all
right.

More surgeries were to follow, and more flights to Cleveland, including one on September 12, 2001. The World Trade Center in New York City
had been attacked the day before, and all flights had been grounded except
for law enforcement and medical emergencies.

"We probably won't be going," said Paul Elzinga, the Wings of Mercy
pilot who was to fly me to Cleveland that day. "But meet me at the airport
just in case."

When I got to Tulip City Airport the doors were locked. A security
guard came over and looked at me like I was crazy. But when Paul showed
up, we were off the ground and up in the air.

We had the sky all to ourselves that day. Not a plane in sight. When we
landed in Cleveland a police escort met us at the ramp and took me to the
hospital. Don't think for a minute that that made me feel important. All I
could feel was the pain in my back.

Unfortunately, my back problems still persist. In a car accident in 2009
I sustained the same injury Christopher Reeve did when he fell off the horse.
I have at least one more major spinal surgery coming.

When you do nothing but suffer for twenty years you turn from the
physical side of your life to the spiritual side. Wings of Mercy has not only
helped me get to and from my surgeries but has helped me grow spiritually
through their compassion for others. I like to tell Pete VandenBosch that
Wings of Mercy should be called "Wings of Grace."

Holly LeBlanc

My story begins as halfway around the world, in Singapore, when I was in
college attending Taylor University's study abroad program. For a young
woman eager to see the world, this was a dream-come-true.

But little by little my dream turned into a nightmare. At first my friends
noticed that my speech was slurring. Then I started having trouble with
balance and muscle coordination. My vision was getting blurred.

By the time I came home to Michigan, I was super sick. The doctors told me I had ataxia, a condition that affects the nervous system, but they didn't know exactly what type it was.

I transferred to Hope College to be closer to home. They finally narrowed my diagnosis to Friedrich's Ataxia, a disease so rare that no treatment had yet been found for it.

Meanwhile, my condition worsened. "Did you sprain your ankle?" people would ask me as I hobbled down the hallway after class. I refused to use a walker because when you're a college student on a walker you can forget about having a social life.

Several years later my sister gave me some information about an organization called the Friedrich's Ataxia Research Alliance. The Alliance was about to undertake a clinical study using a smoking-cessation drug, Chantix, to see if it would cure Friedrich's Ataxia, a disease that had nothing to do with smoking.

The study was to take place in Tampa, Florida, at the Ataxia Research Center of the University of Southern Florida. I applied on a whim, not thinking anything would come of it. When they accepted me I realized I had no way to get to Florida.

A friend's husband told me, "Holly, you should look into Wings of Mercy." I did, and a week later they accepted me, too. Once a month they fly me down to Tampa for several hours of tests at the Ataxia Research Center. They even let me take my service dog, Delsie, on the plane.

November of 2009 marked a turning point for me. My friend Ann flew down with me. It was evident that my speech had improved since my last visit. When the researcher had me run through a word test, Ann started to cry. "I've never heard you talk that way, Holly!" she said.

Apparently all my attention was focused on the test, because I wasn't aware that the room was full of doctors. On my next visit one of them said, "I was there when your friend cried."

Then he paused and said, "In fact we all cried."

Debbi Montambo

W hen my daughter Becki was two, she sustained a head injury from an accidental fall. At first it appeared to be minor, but then she started having seizures. Doctors discovered she had a calcium deposit on her left brain lobe.

Becki would have between one and ten *petit mal* seizures a day, most of them barely noticeable. By the time she was eight, her seizures got worse. She would stop talking in mid-sentence and stare off into space and her eyes would spin around like a clock. Sometimes she would lapse into unconsciousness.

When my husband, Terry, was on a church mission trip Becki had her worst seizure yet. A string of tests ensued. After my husband returned from his mission trip we took our daughter to the doctor's office to find out the results. That was on a Friday.

The doctor told us to sit down before he gave us the news. He had found a tumor in Becki's brain and wasn't able to treat it. He called the Mayo Clinic in Rochester, Minnesota, and scheduled an appointment for Becki the following Tuesday. We knew it was urgent.

On our way home we called from a restaurant to make plane reservations. Round-trip tickets would cost $1,500. We couldn't afford it. We were at a loss for what to do. Back in the car we heard a public service announcement from Wings of Mercy. It was like hearing God's voice on the radio. I wrote down the phone number.

As soon as we got home I called the number. Pete VandenBosch picked up the phone. "I will fly you there myself," he said. On Sunday we met him at Muskegon Airport and he flew us to Rochester.

The children at Mayo come from all over the world. Becki's roommate came from Greece. There was even a child from Iquitos, Peru, where my husband had gone on his mission trip.

On Tuesday Becki had her surgery. The doctor had warned us of possible side effects, such as loss of her peripheral vision. Afterwards he snapped his fingers on the left side of her head and then on the right. Each time Becki turned to look. Her peripheral vision was intact. "You can do anything but bungee jump," the doctor said.

On Friday twenty people greeted us at the Muskegon Airport. "Pete VandenBosch, who had flown back to Rochester to bring us home, said, "Young lady, there's your welcoming committee."

Becki showed off a t-shirt we had bought for her at the Mall of America. It had a picture of her in an angel's outfit with the words, "God's Greatest Miracle."

Joe White

My wife Jill and I were getting ready to go to Italy for her brother's wedding. We were all packed up and ready to go along with my wife's two young children from her previous marriage.

When I woke up my eyes and skin were the color of a yellow legal pad. My wife rushed me to the doctor.

"It looks like your gall bladder is plugged," he said. "But I want the University of Michigan Hospital to confirm the diagnosis."

We canceled our trip to Italy and drove to Ann Arbor. There the doctor inserted an endoscope down my throat to the liver. "I'm afraid I have bad news," he said.

The diagnosis was cholangiocarcinoma, the same type of liver cancer that took Chicago Bears football great Walter Payton and Hall of Fame baseball broadcaster Ernie Harwell. The doctor told me that without a new liver I had a short time to live. He called the Mayo Clinic.

Two days later—thanks to Wings of Mercy—we were on the ground in Rochester, Minnesota. But we were anxious about what would happen next.

A social worker warned us that my life was about to change. "You need to grieve your old life," she said. "You need to find a new normal." Those were awful words to hear.

When I began my chemotherapy my life did indeed change. I had to quit smoking. Then Jill had to quit working so she could care for me full time. Our only income was my monthly disability check.

Twenty-seven more flights to Mayo followed over the next three years. While I waited for a liver transplant my weight dropped from one-hundred eighty pounds to one-hundred thirty-two. I knew that without a new liver the end could be around the corner. All I could do was wait.

Despite the anxiety, we managed to laugh. When we needed some color in our day, one of Jill's kids would point to me and say, "Who's that yellow fellow?" And the other one would reply, "Why, that's Mr. White!"

Finally the long-awaited call came from Rochester: "We have a match."

It took Wings of Mercy all of twenty minutes to arrange a flight. It was a gray January day when we took off. When we approached Rochester a hole opened in the sky and we saw the Mayo Clinic in the bright sunlight. My wife turned to me and said, "That's our color for the day."

Three years later I'm back at work, I have adopted Jill's children as my own, and I have a clean bill of health. Thanks to the people at Mayo and Wings of Mercy, I'm finding a "new normal."

Autumn Peterson

The day after my tenth birthday I was diagnosed with diabetes, but that didn't stop me from playing softball. I started pitching in grade school and was good at it. When I was thirteen I passed out right in the middle of a game. It was 90 degrees outside.

The next thing I knew I was in the back seat of an air conditioned car being administered candy and soft drinks to get my blood sugar up.

Diabetes is hard enough to cope with when you're a rebellious adolescent. It made sleepovers really hard; I didn't want my friends telling me what to eat and not to eat, and I didn't want my parents telling their parents what to do in case something happened to me. Sometimes I just refused to take my insulin.

But then I was diagnosed with sclerosis of the kidney, which made matters worse. Even so, when I got married I was determined to have children. At age twenty-one I lost my first baby during premature delivery. My second baby miscarried at two months. My third baby was a miracle. Colin Joseph was born two months premature but survived. I had him by C-section.

After Colin was born my kidneys got worse. Every four days I would have to go to the hospital for four hours of dialysis. I knew I would have to have a kidney transplant. I got on the transplant waiting list at the University of Wisconsin Hospital in Madison. But it was an all-day drive from my home in Ludington, Michigan. How was I going to get there when they found a donor kidney? A nurse put me in touch with Wings of Mercy.

My husband, Drew, and I had just moved into a new apartment when the phone rang at three o'clock in the morning on the fourth of January, 2008. It was the University of Wisconsin Hospital calling to say they had a kidney for me. Could I come right away?

The plane couldn't take off because of an ice storm, so a Wings of Mercy volunteer offered to drive me all the way around Lake Michigan to Madison, Wisconsin. Imagine that! We were about an hour on the road when the cell phone rang. It was the transplant unit calling to say there was a problem with the kidney. We turned around and went home.

Once again I waited for the phone to ring. The next call came at ten o'clock on the night of January 8. Things happened quickly. I called Wings of Mercy and went straight to the airport. Three hours after the phone call I was in the hospital being prepped for surgery.

The transplant hasn't solved all my problems. I've had to go back to Madison several times because of complications, but I no longer live in fear of death. I'm currently going to West Shore Community College studying medical office information systems. I figure since I've dealt with so many doctors in my life why not work for one?

I have almost died a dozen times, but for some reason God wants me to be here. And I'm grateful to Wings of Mercy for making that possible.

Wings of Mercy pilots receive no payment to fly patients on life-saving medical missions. They do it as volunteers, and often they foot their own fuel costs. Their reward may be a hug or a kiss on the cheek or a thank-you note. Here's a sampling of the thousands of thank yous they have received from grateful patients and their families:

DEAR EARTH ANGELS,

It is hard for me to put into words. Money was never mentioned to me in any way. My trip to the Mayo Clinic was wonderful. One's faith in human kindness is certainly restored.

A PATIENT

I will always think of you as angels of mercy. There will never be enough money to repay you for your time and gift of life to our child.

A PARENT

Thank you for taking our precious grandson to the hospital in Green Bay, Wisconsin, so he could have his heart checked. You are the tangible arms of Jesus.

GRANDPARENTS

I will never be able to express my heart in words on how much I appreciate your service during my trip to the clinic. Yet I do know that God has created angels on earth.

A PATIENT

My family and I all thank you and pray the good Lord will fly with Wings of Mercy, my "Earth Angels," in all their future flights.

A PATIENT

We were faced with a painful pressing need when we learned of Wings of Mercy. You lifted the burden with a cheerful, reassuring "We'll be there! Give us a day and hour!" And you were there! Frankly, I think you are angels.

A PATIENT

Not all thank yous come in the form of hugs or handwritten notes. Wings of Mercy pilot and board member Rob Becker received this poem from a grateful patient:

ANGELS IN FLIGHT

BY JENNIFER K. SMITH

Have you ever had this happen to you,
During the night as you slept in bed?
You wake up with a jumping jolt,
Thoughts spinning in your head?

Perhaps you do as I have done
After waking up once more.
Did a car drive by or a dog bark,
Or is someone at the door?

After many long sleepless nights
Of tossing here and about,
I think I have found the answer.
Yes—I've finally figured it out!

The answer came while returning home from flight
With Wings of Mercy, some very dear friends,
While high up in the mighty sky,
As I looked below the lights didn't end.

That's when it happened,
The realization of my plight,
That Angels never sleep,
As they are constantly in flight.

The answer that I recognized
 Has always been right there.
When I awaken in the night,
The Angels need my help with prayers.

For someone is always hurting,
Needing love and receiving none,
And I'm Blessed to have Our Lord,
God's only begotten Son.

And so I pray for that somebody,
Who may not know our Lord,
And I ask the Angels to deliver the hope
That only prayers can bring forward.

In my prayers I remember
The sick and the dying,
The poor and hungry people,
The lonely that just stop trying.

Somewhere out there in this world
A message of hope will get through,
And, oh how exciting it is to think
That we helped, that's us, me and you!

If not for Wings of Mercy,
The answer would still be unknown,
But since I was on that plane that night,
With many Angels I have flown.

I can never thank Wings of Mercy enough
For flying me around.
They are also beautiful Angels
Both in flight and on the ground!

So, when you have this happen
In the middle of the night,
Just remember it's the Angels beckoning help
To carry our precious prayers in flight.

PART FOUR

Giving Back

Our volunteer pilots are among the greatest group of givers I have ever known. In my book each one is an angel of mercy. Here a few of the 300 pilots who have flown Wings of Mercy missions over the first twenty years describe what the experience has meant to them.

Jeff Ostrander

It is hard to describe the unique role that a Wings of Mercy pilot plays. At the most basic level we are cab drivers, because a vehicle is needed and somebody has to drive it. But somewhere between "hello" and "goodbye" things change.

We, the pilots, have an advantage in our relationship with the patients we transport. We know something of the suffering and danger that our passengers are experiencing. We know that every smile on their face, every cheerful word, is an act of bravery, a picture of courage. As pilots, our immediate questions are about this flight: how much fuel and how much weather. Their questions are more profound; "Will we be able to afford treatment?" "Will my child survive?" They rise from unfathomable depths to meet us at the surface. Or, perhaps, they descend.

I remember one young man, his body by then reduced to a rickety skeleton by the cancer that had nearly consumed him. I was with him for but a few hours on a single day, and yet I was present at two major events in his life. In the morning, I stood awkwardly aside as he said goodbye to friends and family in Michigan where he had spent his adult life. In the afternoon, I stood aside again, an awkward witness as his parents took him gently from the airplane and helped him into an old pickup truck. The reunion, they all knew, was to be brief. He had come home to die. If he spoke a word to me, I do not remember it, but I will always remember the steady gaze from his exhausted face, the kindly nod to say, "Thanks. I'm okay."

Does God waste pain? Is our suffering ever for nothing? Is crisis a private thing—a virus to be hidden and quarantined? As I have watched the patients and families served by Wings of Mercy I have seen something very different: that families and friends can bear a little of the burden, can help to answer a question deeper than "How will we get to the hospital?" or "What will this disease do to me?"

I am just a cabbie but I carry in my heart and in my flying a little of God's love for these brave people. Thanks to Peter VandenBosch, I can be a part of the answer to their deeper question: "Is there a love and purpose for my life that transcends even this illness?" It is to answer this question that Wings of Mercy exists: to share another's burdens, sometimes to weep with those who weep, always to say with our service that God is here, that his love and mercy reach into every dark corner of this hard world.

Jerry Schmidt

I was flying in clear weather toward Michigan's Upper Peninsula en route from Ann Arbor to Houghton, Michigan, late in the afternoon as the cancer patient's appointment at the University of Michigan's Medical Center took longer than expected. It was beautiful watching the sun get lower in the sky. Near Traverse City the clouds covered the landscape below us. Soon we were in a valley of clouds with mountains of clouds on both sides of us. Then a rainbow appeared in distance; it seemed a sure sign that the Lord was with us on this flight.

As we continued, the clouds rose higher and it began to snow. My copilot and I watched vigilantly for any sign of ice to form on the wings. When it started to form I requested to descend to warmer air below us. I glanced back to see if our passengers were concerned. The cancer patient and his wife were smiling. I don't know if they sensed God's presence, but I could see they had confidence in the plane and our skills as pilots.

Our trip plan was toward an area of precipitation showing on the GPS screen. We reminded the passengers to keep their seat belts tight as there would probably be some turbulence ahead. To avoid the heaviest rain we deviated further north than our direct course. Soon we were over the shore line of Lake Superior. It was time to turn into the weather. I prayed that the ride would continue to be smooth. The radar showed areas of green and yellow depicting moderate rain. To a pilot, moderate rain usually means a bumpy ride and for this reason I don't like to fly into areas of moderate rain.

It was time to discuss our options with my co-pilot. We agreed that we had three options: We could land and wait for the rain to blow through (that would put us into a nighttime flight which is not permitted by Wings of Mercy policy for a single engine flight), turn back to a larger city which would mean we would need to stay in a hotel for the night, or continue on while evaluating conditions as we flew. We decided to continue while leaving all options open to us at any time.

Again the Lord showed his hand. As we flew toward the precipitation it started to dissipate. By the time we entered the area of rain showers they were nearly gone. It was a smooth ride and soon we started our descent to the Houghton airport. Our passengers were home. As we retrieved their luggage and walked into the terminal with them, they expressed thanks and kindness.

It is humbling to only help one patient at a time. I wish we could do much more. We do know that if we can help even one it makes our time on this earth worthwhile. I always know we are being prayed for on each flight. The Lord does many wonders to demonstrate His care for us as we fly.

Gary Sage

It was 1994 and I had just begun flying for Wings of Mercy. I had flown a few patients to the Mayo Clinic in Rochester, Minnesota, and was new to this. I was observing the differences between patients, outwardly some appeared very sick, others did not. I often thought about their lives and why some people are struggling with health issues all of their lives and others only have to worry about the occasional cold.

On one particular flight I flew a patient that I would never forget. It began as a standard request: "Could you fly to Cleveland, pick up a patient and bring him home to his family in Lansing for Thanksgiving? He is not doing well in the nursing home and the family would like to spend time with him." Sure, I said, I can take the flight."

A few days later we departed Grand Rapids Gerald R. Ford International Airport for a morning flight. At 9,000 feet the sky was clear and nothing out of the ordinary was forecast. It was going to be a smooth flight. When we arrived at the Cleveland airport, I was met by an aging gentleman and his nurse. Using a walker, he walked slowly toward the airplane. His nurse pushed the oxygen caddy that gave him the ability to breathe, using the lungs that were crippled with emphysema. After loading everyone in the airplane and going through the preflight briefing, we took off for Lansing, Michigan. So far this was another flight, just like the others; the flight was smooth and the patient was doing well.

When we landed, the patient's family was at the FBO waiting for us. Everyone from daughters and sons to grandchildren, and even great grandchildren, were there to greet their loved one. They all thanked the co-pilot and me for bringing him home to be with them over Thanksgiving, with one exception…the patient. He did not have enough lung capacity to speak, but as he turned to sit down in the back seat of their car we made eye contact, and at that moment I saw a more loving "Thank you for bringing me home to my family" than mere words could ever describe. It stopped me in my tracks. I could not move, and all I could say was, "You are so welcome." It was a solemn flight back. I could not stop thinking about that look and the family reunion they must be having now. Two weeks later I received a letter at my office. It was from the family. John had died the week after we dropped him off at the airport. The family wanted me to know how much it meant to them to have their dad with them for the few remaining days he had left. I will always remember how much their father's "Thank you" meant to me and what a special Thanksgiving that was for me.

Kevin Dingman

This story first appeared December 2010 in Twin and Turbine magazine and is reprinted with permission:

"I introduced a young man to aviation; infected him I did. In 1988 I was in the Air Force and one weekend a buddy and I took two F-16's cross country to Michigan. Michael, along with a crowd of friends and relatives, met the two F-16's on arrival. It was an exciting day for him and all the folks that had never been this close to a real Air Force fighter. Michael was hooked.

"When my career finally led me back home to Michigan, Michael was there. My friend was now all grown up. He was married with children, a college graduate, and an Airframe & Powerplant mechanic as well as an instrument flight instructor. He had swallowed it all, hook, line and tie-down chain.

"I'd purchased a Beechcraft Duke only a few months before moving back home. Michael had mentioned to me several times he was involved with a Christian organization that flew people to appointments at medical facilities that, for a variety of reasons, couldn't use the airlines or highways. Michael would be my co-pilot and mechanic. The pieces were falling into place.

"I have since flown dozens of missions for Wings of Mercy. Some patients were children and some were adults. Some old, some young. Some have since passed away. A few recovered. After one flight, as the patient and his wife were getting off the plane and gathering their things, they came to thank me. Here was this very polite and articulate terminally ill man—thanking me for flying an airplane. The thing I love to do. I have never been so embarrassed and ashamed at the same time in my life.

"My life is so easy. I have everything anyone could want. My flying career has been everything you could hope for—fighter Pilot, airline pilot, airplane owner. Here is a terminally ill man and his wife thanking me—*them* thanking *me*. I was a fighter pilot. "There is no such thing as humble when you're a fighter pilot. Like a Band-Aid being ripped off quickly, the Lord made me humble in an instant. No suffering along the way, amazing.

'The gentleman passed away shortly after he flew with us. His wife is now alone — and my comfortable life goes on. Over the next few missions I had to learn to not choke up when the patient shows us gratitude."

From that thank you forward, I'm different. I'm more relaxed and happy. Thank you, Michael, for introducing me to the Wings of Mercy family. Thank you, Peter VandenBosch, for founding Wings of Mercy, reuniting old friends, and providing the environment for me to learn "humble."

Jay Van Daalen

The flight involved a homeless man who needed to get from Grand Rapids to Cleveland for back surgery. It was on a Sunday morning. We flew from Holland to Grand Rapids, taxied up to the FBO and he was there ready to go. All he had were the clothes on his back and a very small bag with just the basic essentials in it. We had an uneventful flight to Cleveland's Burke Lakefront Airport, dropped him off and returned to Holland. He had the surgery and other Wings pilots returned him to Grand Rapids at a later date. The reason for telling about this is that for three years after the flight on that anniversary Sunday of the flight he would call me at home and thank me again for the flight that enabled him to have the special surgery that he needed. There is no way I can ever forget this man. He may have been homeless, without a job or a cent to his name, but he was a thoughtful, grateful and gracious person.

By the very nature of what we were doing, most of the flights were for people who had run out of options for treatment in Western Michigan and were going to Mayo Clinic, or some such place, hoping that they could discover a diagnoses or a treatment plan for an often life threatening situation. We picked up a couple in Northern Michigan and took them to Rochester, Minnesota. He was probably in his fifties, and had been given six months to live. He had been told that there was nothing that they could do for him that already hadn't been done. He was going to Mayo hoping that they would have something new or different that would prolong his life. As it turned out I was also the PIC on their return flight. When we met them at the airport in Rochester the first thing we wanted to know was how it went and what did they find out. They calmly stated that there was nothing that could be done for him, quickly followed by a genuine gratefulness to us for the opportunity to have his situation explored at a leading medical center. Everything possible had been done so they could be at peace with his end of life.

We once took a single gal in her early twenties to Rochester. She had been diagnosed with a difficult cancer at Mayo a year or so before and had been sent home with a treatment plan. She was told in Michigan that the cancer was now in remission and she was returning to Mayo for a check up and confirmation. We got there and her transportation to the clinic was delayed so we shared our lunch with her at the table in the FBO lounge. After we had eaten I got up, paid the fuel bill and then the copilot and I said our goodbyes to her and best wishes for a good report. Her response was, "Where do you think you're going? I was a little taken back but responded that we were returning to Holland. She said, "Not until I give each of you a big hug." It was one of those things that are etched in my memory for life.

John Workman

On Christmas, just before my fortieth birthday, my wife gave me a present: the "Blue Sky Special," a thirty-minute introductory flight class. Forty-two flying hours later I had my pilot's license.

My business had succeeded to the point where I had some discretionary income. I bought a Piper Warrior, a single engine aircraft, and flew it as often as I could for business and pleasure. Later I upgraded to a Piper Saratoga, a single-engine six-seater.

On a flight to Nebraska I ran into a snowstorm. The engine started to freeze up, and I had to make an emergency landing in St. Louis. There I was stranded for several days. When I got home I decided to upgrade. I wanted a plane with de-icing capacity and a pressurized cabin that would enable me to fly above the weather. So in 1995 I bought a twin-engine eight-seat Cessna 414.

Meanwhile, a friend of my father's had put me in touch with Pete VandenBosch. When Pete told me about his organization on the phone, I suggested we meet in person. We met at the Brownstone Restaurant at the Muskegon Airport. When Pete told me the Wings of Mercy story, I got hooked. I had served on the boards of several nonprofit organizations, but here was an opportunity to help people on a personal basis. I agreed on the spot to become a Wings of Mercy pilot. Since then I have flown over two hundred thirty missions and logged more than a thousand hours as a volunteer pilot.

Many of the patients have made a deep impression on me. One of them was a baby born prematurely in Newberry, a small town in Michigan's Upper Peninsula. The closest adequate care she could get was in Grand Rapids. After living apart from her parents for the first year of her life, the little girl was finally able to go home. It was my privilege to deliver her to her parents. What a reunion that was!

Another patient was a young man I flew from Muskegon to the University of Michigan Medical Center in Ann Arbor for treatment of brain cancer. I'll never forget what his mother told me afterwards: "We went down with a thimbleful of hope and came back with a bucketful."

Giving hope to people is why I fly for Wings of Mercy. The experience is humbling. Flying for them keeps me grounded.

Gary Vander Veen

Pete's belief that it really was God talking to him on that boat off the coast of Naples to start flying people with needs was an example of his faith. I've always thought that Pete was more inclined to believe it really was a message from above because he is a pilot. After all, pilots can't physically see the lift that supports their wings. But starting with the Wright brothers we believe this lift thing that Bernoulli's principle described will get us up and away. And of course, when we fly God doesn't have to yell as hard at us to get our attention, because we're closer to Him.

Wings of Mercy patients are faith-filled flyers as well. Sometimes they may be a little nervous about getting in the "little airplane." However, their need and their faith get them on board. Wings of Mercy crews, with their professionalism, good judgment, superior flying skills and empathy for first-time "little airplane" flyers all help to nurture the patient's faith.

One of the perks of being a Wings pilot is to experience the genuine gratefulness expressed by the passengers. The sales guys who I fly around professionally don't give me a hug at the end of the flight, but Wings' patients often times do. To be the "get there fast" component along with medical professionals, family, friends and church members who are all help-ing to improve, heal, extend and provide comfort for this patient's life is an honor.

I've always said that the best example for pilots to follow is the servant attitude of Jesus Christ. I'm not talking about airline pilots here that get to close the door and let the flight attendants handle it. I'm talking about ser-vant pilots who give of their time, empty the potty, dispose of the barf bags, comfort the "nervous Nellie", are on call for the kidney transplant, and freeze their butts off at Rochester on a winter time Mayo run.

My first patient flight for Wings left me a changed man. I called Pete and said, "Thank you for letting me do this mission. It changed me from being so very selfish."

Nick Jilek

It started out as a typical flight for Wings of Mercy. Gary and I landed at the departure airport several minutes prior to our patient and passenger's arrival, allowing us to follow our normal routine — where I check out the aircraft and take on fuel, while Gary gets an update on the weather.

Today our patient looks vaguely familiar, although I can't place her, and I don't recognize the passenger. During conversation prior to boarding the aircraft, we learn our patient is traveling with her daughter, and we're tak-ing them home to southern Indiana. We have flown this patient before — but this time the news is not good. Her body has rejected the transplant, and she is going home to spend her final days with her family.

We have a smooth flight, an above minimums instrument approach and landing, and although unfamiliar with the small airport where we landed, there is no doubt where we will be parking the aircraft. There are dozens of relatives awaiting our arrival, many carrying large "Welcome Home" banners.

Was this a joyous flight, filled with promise and hope? Probably not, given the prognosis, but it did have a happy ending, with our travelers lit-erally being welcomed with open arms by family and friends.

One may ask, "Why do we do this?" The answers are as complex as they are simple. Yes, as pilots we prefer the flights where the prognosis for the patient is good, and I'm sure the patient prefers this also! However, be it an infant in need of special care, cradled in Mom or Dad's arms, or a hard-scrabble farmer from out west, who never depended on anyone else in his life and is embarrassed to ask for help, our job, indeed, our calling, is to make them feel at home; to make them as comfortable as possible; to do everything we can to help.

In a nutshell, we do this to help; we do this to give back. There are many ways to serve others and we are doing our best to use the skills we have in the best manner possible. Thank you, thank you to Wings of Mercy for providing the tools to enable us to do this.

Carl Walker

I had never heard of Wings of Mercy until I flew our Beech Baron to Bay City on a Saturday Morning a number of years ago to do some recurrent training. I don't recall the instructor's name. However, we went up and did the usual stuff, holding patterns, approaches, etc. While in the air, he asked me if I had heard of Wings of Mercy and told me that he was check pilot for them. He then pulled some papers out of his flight bag, wrote on them, told me that I had been approved as a Wings pilot, and asked me to contact the office in Holland, which I did. Thus, I began my flying with Wings of Mercy.

The relationships with the Wings SIC pilots has been one of the high points of the Wings flying experience — new friends from the Holland and Grand Rapids areas, Traverse City, and the flight school students from Western Michigan University. Then, there is the Wings of Mercy administration. They are the tops. Sharon and Grace do a wonderful job, particularly with the midnight phone calls regarding flying a transplant patient to an organ source.

Wings of Mercy would not have happened without Peter, and the other fund raisers which allow the pilots to fly without digging as much into their own pockets. It's all one Christ directed team.

Last, but most moving, are the experiences with the patients. They are a wonderful group. To see them go to medical centers like Mayo Clinic with their health concerns, and come home with hope. I'll always remember one young woman, a bit over weight with two elementary school children, and who went to Mayo for a second opinion. Paul and I went back to Rochester to pick her up a few days later. She was rather subdued on the return trip. I finally got up the nerve to ask her how things went. She broke down in tears, then got a big smile on her face, and said, "I went to Mayo expecting the worst. They said that my local doctor had prescribed the correct tests and I didn't have to go through any more tests at Mayo. They gave me a medication list and said I had to lose some weight, and I should have a good life ahead." Now, isn't that what Wings of Mercy is all about? Praise the Lord!

Tim Brutsche

I have been lucky to have had the privilege to participate in approximately 100 Wings flights, either as PIC or as SIC. Each and every flight has had a story; every one special in its own way. I have gone back and looked through my logbook, piecing together the chronology of the flights, remembering the patients. While a couple come to mind easier because of multiple trips, like a gentleman from Ludington who had skin cancer, and made numerous flights to Mayo Clinic. (He sent me a personal letter before he passed away, telling me how the flights had given him a couple more years on this earth). Many of the short, one time trips are just as easy to recall because the patients were so special. While the patient "got a flight" out of me, I received much more in return from them. Not money or gifts; it was their attitude that amazed me. Many of these individuals were excited about going to receive a treatment that might save their lives, so their excitement was understandable. Many others were coming home after receiving the news that they were going to die, but were equally happy knowing they had fought the good fight, and were coming home to friends and family. I do not know if I could be as brave as these individuals are, especially the children who have not seen a full life.

I know I am a better person because of flying for Wings of Mercy. I know (while you will not read it in the newspapers or find a statistic citing the fact) I have made a difference in the lives of others. It isn't something I need to stand up at a podium and announce — it's between me and the "Big Guy" upstairs.

We need to keep this "thing" called Wings of Mercy going and growing. Those of us who are lucky enough to be blessed with the ability to fly can make a difference in this world. Call it "pay it forward" or even "pay back", it's simply the right thing to do.

Russ McNamara

I first learned about Wings of Mercy through the newspaper. An informal meeting at the Park Place in Traverse City was advertised in the newspaper and I decided to attend. I was initially interested because I love to fly. After all, every day is a great day to fly. During the meeting I realized this was something I wanted to be a part of. Not just because I would get to fly, but because it could help make a difference in people's lives. Additionally, Peter VandenBosch is one of the very few people in this world that you just cannot say "NO" to. Especially after he just bought you lunch. So without hesitation, I signed up and flew my first mission. I enjoyed it and could see immediately what Peter was talking about. Now, 15 years later I have flown over 150 missions and look forward to completing many more.

Each mission is unique, special and equally as important as the next. Sometimes we fly to familiar hospitals like Mayo Clinic or to a children's hospital or to more specialized treatment centers. We fly because we truly enjoy helping these everyday heroes; we are simply aiding them in their fight against tremendous odds. It is our hope that through Wings of Mercy, we are able to save some time, even save some money for people who are just trying to survive or simply better their quality of life. Without Wings of Mercy, some of these individuals would not be able to travel long distances to see the doctors they need to see. In some cases, air transportation through general aviation is the only option because if they were to drive a car for ten-plus hours, it would be simply excruciating as compared to a two hour or less flight. Perhaps the biggest reason why I love to fly for Wings of Mercy is to see the mothers, fathers and other relatives who accompany the ill with huge smiles on their faces. It is at this moment that I realize we are not just helping one person, but an entire family.

It is with great pleasure and honor that I serve these everyday heroes and look forward to all of my flights for Wings of Mercy, not just one, because it is the large number of individuals that we get to help each year that is extraordinary. Any pilot can fly someone to a hospital, but we, the pilots of Wings of Mercy, fly hundreds each year. We are blessed to be their pilot and know that each one of us, if asked, could not isolate one person they enjoyed more than another. We enjoy helping them all. So here we stand, willing and ready to help in the time of need.

Mark Evans

Peter, I was approached by one of your other Earth Angels, Russ McNamara, to consider joining this wonderful group of caring pilots. Initially, I thought it would be a great way to increase my time aloft, but after taking my first trip with Russ it became apparent that there was a bigger mission here than my needs. A small child that was born with numerous birth defects was my first passenger, and after being told she would never walk, I was blessed after flying her and her mom several times, to see her walk down a FBO lobby with the aid of a walker. After clearing the moisture from my eyes, God revealed his power and glory to me. God bless you and the Wings of Mercy.

Dave Siegers

One Wings of Mercy flight that was particularly memorable to me was when we flew from Holland, Michigan to Sault Ste. Marie in the Upper Peninsula, to pick up a mother and her teenage son. He had an appointment at the University of Michigan hospital in Ann Arbor for a serious illness. We waited for his appointment to be over and then flew the two of them home again before returning to Holland.

In previous flights for Wings I experienced how grateful patients were, and how humbling and touching it was. They feel so blessed and yet they have no idea what a blessing they are to us pilots. This flight was all that and more. This time I could identify with the mother. I could see the anxiety in her eyes and sense her pain for her son. You see, I know what it is like to lose a teenage son because my son Kyle was tragically killed in a car accident a few months earlier. I didn't share my story with her because she had her own problems to handle, but I had a new appreciation for what she was going through. With my heightened compassion for hurting people, no Wings flight will ever be the same. God has blessed me in so many ways, and now I want to be a blessing to others, and Wings of Mercy is a way for me to do that. I'm grateful to Wings for the opportunity.

Albert E. Sickinger

My desire to fly goes back to when I graduated from high school, but I did not realize that dream until 1975 when due to the fuel crisis speed limits in Michigan were reduced from 70 M.P.H. to 55 M.P.H. Suddenly the weekend drive from Bloomfield Hills, Michigan to our cottage Up North became drudgery. Flying reduced the four hour plus drive to one hour twenty minutes. When I sold the business of manufacturing machinery for mechanical loose leaf binding, my flying hours dropped from two hundred hours per year to eighty. In a complex airplane that is not enough to stay proficient even with annual retraining at a flight school.

While discussing my hours with the manager of maintenance at Michigan Aviation in Pontiac one day, he asked if I would be interested in flying for Wings of Mercy. In order to find out, I applied and had my first flight taking a little nine year old, twenty five pound girl and her parents from Alpena, Michigan to Gaithersburg, Maryland. It was my first cross county flight with a copilot and sort of a check out flight by a board member of Wings of Mercy East Michigan. That trip got me hooked. This little girl had such huge medical problems, yet never complained and always had a smile on her face. Hope was her name, and I flew her many more times after that.

Then, there was a relay flight with Wings of Mercy Minnesota transporting an infant to Montreal. A pick up in Boston of another little girl and parents delivered to Saginaw, Michigan, and children from Hancock, Michigan to Ann Arbor followed. One adult cancer patient was taken from Houghton Lake, Michigan to Waukegan, Illinois, a one hour fifteen minute flight which would have taken many hours by any other means of transportation. That is the reason why Wings of Mercy is of such benefit to the patients. In all the missions flown, no patient, child or adult, has ever complained about their problems. As we get older we all have some problems, be it arthritis or something else, but transporting all these grateful people has made me realize that my ailments are nothing compared to the patients we fly with Wings of Mercy.

Not all trips are happy ones. There have been cancer patients getting their last flight home because there is nothing more the hospital can do for them. We strive to make this last flight as comfortable as possible.

I have now flown about 220 missions for Wings of Mercy (east and west) over the last 10 years. Somewhere down the road I, too, will have to retire from flying, but I will have many memories of very gratifying hours flying for Wings of Mercy.

Peter VandenBosch

It was Christmas Eve afternoon, 1991, when I received an emergency call from a Muskegon, Michigan hospital stating that they had a low income four year old girl who had a brain tumor and needed to be flown to Mayo Clinic in Rochester, Minnesota immediately. I accepted.

I was ordered by her doctor not to fly above 6,000 feet because of air pressure. Over the Mississippi River the young father tapped me on the shoulder stating that his little daughter's temperature had climbed to 105 degrees. He asked what they should do, land here at Lacrosse, Wisconsin, or proceed to Rochester, which was 11 minutes away. I told him he and his wife must make that decision. They chose Rochester.

I declared an emergency and was cleared to land on the runway of my choice. I selected runway 20 and requested an ambulance to meet us on the runway. It was granted, and as soon as we landed the medics got her on life support. We said goodbyes, and we then returned to Holland, Michigan. The next day, Christmas Day (my wife's birthday) at 10:30 in the morning we got a call from the father, after her admission and surgery, saying, "We have witnessed a Christmas miracle. She is sitting on her bed playing." She then went on to complete grade school, graduate from high school and Michigan State University. I will never forget this mercy flight.

And again I wish to thank all the Wings of Mercy pilots (PIC and SIC) who in my opinion "are among the greatest group of givers I ever experienced in my life."

EARTH ANGELS
VOLUNTEER ORGANIZATIONS

You don't have to be a pilot to give back. If you are looking for an opportunity to volunteer, the following national and international organizations may interest you:

GOOD NEWS FOR ASIA

Good News for Asia is Mission Organization intent on "Spreading the Gospel of Jesus Christ throughout Asia." Billions of people do not know Him in this area of the world!

Good News for Asia (GNFA) carries out its mandate in three main ways. One is by planting and watering churches. Currently we employ over 100 indigenous pastors and missionaries! Secondly, we now have Children's Homes serving over 70 children in India. Also, GNFA's vision is to build Christian Schools, and we have three active Christian English Medium Schools, one with the capability of admitting 1,200 students. Along with these three main focus points, when other needs arise, we do relief work to wipe away the tears of the poor and needy.

Contact: David Kapteyn. 1.616.748.6070 or www.goodnewsforasia.com

KIDS HOPE USA

KID HOPE USA has a singular mission: we teach churches to mentor at-risk public elementary school children whose ability to learn is seriously impaired by emotional and social issues over which they have no control. Launched in February, 1995, KHUSA has mobilized nearly 1000 churches in the United States and Australia to engage their members in one-to-one, I-believe-in-you relationships with 13,500 vulnerable children. These relationships impact children and adults. The children care to learn when they know that someone cares about them; mentors report their faith is strengthened as they make a difference in one child's life.

Contact: Virgil Gulker. 1.616.546.3580 or vgulkerkidshopeusa.org

LIVING WATER INTERNATIONAL

A child dies of a water-related disease every 15 seconds. You can do something about it. Clean water changes everything. Living Water International exists to demonstrate the love of God by helping communities acquire desperately needed clean water, and to experience "living water"- the gospel of Jesus Christ - which alone satisfies the deepest thirst. We need your help. Give, engage your friends, volunteer, or even go on a trip to drill a well yourself.

Contact: Judi Mohney. www.water.cc or jodiwater.cc

GLOW MINISTRIES INTERNATIONAL

GLOW is an acronym for God's Love for Orphans and Widows. GLOW was formed to share the blessing with the most destitute of Haiti. We established a network of leaders from the local Haitian communities who have poured themselves into positive development in Haiti. They live the culture and understand its limitations. While they have established the ground work in their respective communities, they struggle for bread to feed the children and potable water that provides health and vitality.

GLOW partners with nine Haitian communities. We serve the local church and support schools with feeding programs and consistent wages for teachers. These programs benefit the entire community, providing income and relieving food insecurity in many homes. These villages represent 3,000 children who attend school and receive a nutritional hot lunch every school day.

GLOW partners with these communities to provide strategic widow and orphan care, medical benevolence and community development.

P.O.Box 123, Zeeland, MI 49464; 1.616.772.3370 or www.glowmi.org

WINGS OF MERCY: HOW CAN I HELP?

Wings of Mercy provides free air transportation for people with limited financial means who need treatment at distant medical facilities. You may help in one of these ways:

- By volunteering to be a Wings of Mercy pilot.
- By supporting Wings of Mercy with your contributions.

For more information, visit our website www.wingsofmercy.org.

Wings of Mercy, Inc.
100 Pine Street
Zeeland, MI 49464
Toll free: 1-888-786-3729
Phone: 616-396-1077
Fax: 616-748-6093

A successful life isn't just about making money. It's about finding the Green Stick—the key to happiness and spiritual fulfillment. Greg Nieuwsma interviewed several people about how they, too, found the Green Stick. Most are retired, some are still working. What they have in common is a desire to give back to society and make a difference. I hope their search inspires yours.

Greg Jackson

Greg is a software designer in Durham, North Carolina, and helps build homes for Habitat for Humanity in New Orleans.

A year after Hurricane Katrina hit New Orleans, the employer I worked for at the time said I had to use or lose my six weeks of accrued vacation time. I went down to New Orleans to help clean up after the hurricane.

The experience changed my life. The volunteers I met came from every walk of life and every race, religion, and socio-economic background. All those differences were erased as we united in a common purpose; to help people whose lives had been devastated by Hurricane Katrina.

Even through a job change and a move to another state, I have returned to New Orleans every fall (save one) to help with the recovery effort. Several years ago I organized a group called the "Hammerheads" to help Habitat for Humanity build homes for families displaced by Katrina. The group is still going strong.

One night after we laid down our hammers I decided to visit Bourbon Street with two of my fellow volunteers. A woman approached us with an armful of hats and shoved one at us demanding a price. My first reaction was to say, "Sorry, we don't need any hats. We're here volunteering with Habitat for Humanity."

The woman withdrew the hat, stepped back, and asked us where we were from and what we were doing. When we told her, she said, "Well, God bless y'all. And thanks for taking time to come all the way down here to help us."

We scratched our heads in bewilderment and continued on our way. When we reached the end of Bourbon Street we turned around and started back. The woman selling the hats stopped in the middle of a transaction to smile and wave at us. A few feet away a man selling hot dogs hollered at us, "Thank you and God bless you!"

Not one other person approached us with something to sell. It seemed that everyone knew who we were and why we were there. From that point on we made an effort to talk with people, to listen to their stories, and to give them a reassuring hug.

Volunteering isn't just about doing something that makes you feel good. It's about helping people feel better about themselves. It's about giving hope to people who feel like they've been forgotten and sharing in their darkness.

But I have to admit, every time I come back I feel better about myself, too.

Want to volunteer for Habitat for Humanity in New Orleans? Go to www.habitat-nola.org. Elsewhere? Go to www.habitat.org.

Deanne Bolt

Deanne is a retired special education teacher and tutors Native American children in New Mexico with her husband Bob.

Several years ago when Bob and I were driving through New Mexico on winter break we passed a sign on Historic Route 66 outside Gallup that said "Rehoboth Christian School."

I remembered the name from my childhood. In Sunday school we used to collect coins for the children of Rehoboth so they could go to school. We called them our Indian "cousins."

We pulled off the highway to check it out. Founded in the early 1900s by missionaries from the Christian Reformed Church, the school serves some four hundred Navajo, Hopi and Zuni children from preschool through the 12th grade. Some travel fifty miles each way by bus.

The campus consists of an old high school with cracks in the floor, a somewhat newer grammar and middle school, computer labs, an observatory, a chapel, and a museum honoring the Navajo code talkers who helped us defeat Japan in World War II. We learned that many of them were Rehoboth graduates.

The following winter we went back as volunteers, and we've been doing it every year since we retired. Besides tutoring, Bob works the lunch line, substitute teaches, and does odd jobs. One day he even helped out in preschool but decided that wasn't his calling.

I work one-on-one with kids who need reading help. The teacher designs the program, and I follow it. I help the younger kids with sight words. After a year or two of individual tutoring, most are on the same reading level as their peers. It's rewarding to see their progress.

Volunteer accommodations aren't the most luxurious, but that doesn't matter. Most of us stay in motel-style guest rooms that include a living area and kitchenette. Some stay in their RVs.

Every Wednesday the volunteers have a social gathering. That's when we find out where everybody comes from and what they're doing at Rehoboth. Their skills range from basic things like glazing windows (which is what Bob's brother did one year) to high-tech things like fixing computers (which is what a couple we met from California did).

We plan to go back next year, and the year after that. When people ask me why we do it, I tell them it's for two reasons: It's useful for the school, and it's fulfilling for us. Apart from seeing our grandchildren, I can't think of a better way to spend our time.

Want to volunteer at Rehoboth Christian School in New Mexico? Go to www.rcsnm.org.

Jim Johnson

Jim is a retired psychology professor and volunteer truck driver for Community Action House in Holland, Michigan.

I grew up in the Chicago area. I came from a Catholic family and lived in a Catholic neighborhood and went to a Catholic school until I was eight.

Then my family moved to Oak Park, a mostly Protestant Chicago suburb that Ernest Hemingway who grew up there described as having "broad lawns and narrow minds." I was one of two or three Catholic children at my school. Kids were told not to talk to me. My girlfriend told her parents I was Episcopalian. I played along with the charade until they pressed me for the name of my "pastor."

Still, I didn't have it as bad as some others. Percy Julian, a renowned chemist and the first African-American to move to Oak Park, had his house firebombed. I remember my father getting out his shotgun and sitting on Julian's front lawn to offer his protection until the police came and sent him home.

After getting my Ph.D. from St. Louis University, I returned to the Chicago area to teach psychology at Loyola University. There I started organizing student volunteer activities including Volunteers Interested in People (VIP), which provided students as a community resource. I also designed a course that gave students credit for community service. Today volunteering is a required part of Loyola's curriculum.

Despite all this organizational work based on psychological theories I espoused, I had never rolled up my own sleeves. When I retired and moved to Michigan I decided it was time to practice what I preached. Through my professional contacts I hooked up with David Myers, a psychology professor at Hope College, who helped found Community Action House in Holland. Community Action House has several programs including a soup kitchen and a transitional housing program for the homeless.

I do some of the administrative work for these programs, but my main job is to drive the Community Action House truck. When there's food to be donated to the soup kitchen I go pick it up. When someone donates furniture I pick it up and deliver it to whoever needs it. Last week I delivered a crib to a single mom.

I was born with a silver spoon in my mouth, but I can relate to hunger. In my case it has been by choice. The people who come to the soup kitchen, they have no choice.

Want to volunteer for Community Action House in Holland, Michigan? Go to www.communityactionhouse.org. Or contact your local chapter of the Salvation Army (www.salvationarmy.org) or Goodwill Industries (www.goodwill.org).

George Greene

George, an environmental engineer, and his wife Molly founded Water Missions International in Charleston, South Carolina.

When I heard on the radio about Hurricane Mitch hitting Honduras in 1998, it meant more to me than it did the average listener. Our daughter had just returned after living there for two years. I felt the need to do something, but I wasn't ready to act.

To ease my conscience I e-mailed the Episcopal bishop in Tegucigalpa, the capital, asking if there was something we could do to help. Knowing that much of the country lacked electricity and how difficult it was to contact my daughter under normal circumstances, I wasn't expecting a response. I thought that would give me the right to say, "Well, I tried."

But you can't outsmart the Lord. To my surprise the bishop replied the next morning to my e-mail. "We need six drinking water units," he said.

That obliged me to act. I started looking for water units, but the only one I could find was a $350,000 military unit. Obviously, that wasn't feasible. So I sat down with some engineers at my company, and with their help I sketched out a crude design for a disaster response water purification system. Then we went to work.

While I was busy on the engineering side, Molly was busy on the logistics side. Through our senator she had arranged for a C-5 plane to fly the units to Honduras. Meanwhile, word had gotten out about what we were doing and all of Charleston got behind the project. People and churches donated fifty tons of materials—food, clothes, medical and building supplies.

When we got to Honduras we were faced with the realities of a disaster area. Roads and bridges had been washed out; bodies were floating in the water. In order to get to the villages to deliver the water units we had to drive through water up to the axles.

The irony of course was that there was water everywhere, but none of it was fit to drink. The river near one village was the color of chocolate milk. The locals called it "The River of Death." When we turned on the newly installed system there, clean water poured out. Not surprisingly, the residents were suspicious. When Molly and I placed our lips to the hose and drank, the villagers surged forward to drink the newly cleansed water.

When we returned to Charleston we decided to branch our business out into emergency water systems. Over the next two years we took on projects in Turkey and Mozambique. But we came to realize two things. One was the scale of the global water crisis; twenty percent of the world's population doesn't have access to clean water. The other was that there was no money to be made in this endeavor. The twenty percent without clean water are among the world's poorest people and obviously have no way to pay for it. The money has to come from somewhere else.

So on the last Saturday in September 2000, Molly and I took the phone off the hook and spent the day talking, praying, reading the Bible. In April we sold our business and started Water Missions International, Inc.

In retrospect, it's clear what God wanted us to do; devote ourselves full-time to providing clean water to the poorest of the poor and people affected by disasters. I believe God endows each of us with a unique talent, and it's our obligation to use that talent to do his will. In my case, it's an engineering skill. In Molly's case it's an organizational skill. Together we're able to make a difference.

Want to volunteer for Water Missions International? Go to www.water-missions.org.

Volunteering is as American as apple pie—and a terrific option for retirement age baby-boomers looking for the Green Stick. According to the Corporation for National and Community Service, more than 64 million Americans volunteered to help their communities in 2009, and the number keeps growing. If you want to volunteer in your community—or farther away from home—here are some websites worth checking out:

AMERICAN RED CROSS. Provides disaster relief through 700 chapters nationwide. A good fit for volunteers who have flexible schedules and a need for an adrenaline rush.

www.redcross.org

EXPERIENCE CORPS. Engages adults 55 and over as literacy tutors for elementary students in 19 cities around the country. Volunteer applicants are individually interviewed, screened, and trained.

www.experiencecorps.org

SENIOR CORPS. A government agency that serves children and senior citizens in need of emotional support, coaching, and help with disabilities. Open to volunteers 55 and over.

www.seniorcorps.gov

PEACE CORPS. A government agency that provides technical assistance to developing countries. Applicants must have a college degree and commit to two years of service abroad.

www.peacecorps.gov

AMERICORPS. A government agency that addresses domestic needs in education, public safety, health, and the environment. Open to volunteers seeking long-term assignments.

www.americorps.gov

GLOBE AWARE. Hosts one-week volunteer "vacation" programs in such places as Peru, Costa Rica, and Ghana for roughly $1,250 per person plus airfare. A good short-term option for families with kids.

www.globeaware.org

UNITED NATIONS VOLUNTEERS. The online volunteering service of the United Nations. Seeks virtual assistance for project development, research, writing, translation, and coaching.

www.onlinevolunteering.org

VOLUNTEER MATCH. Matches volunteers with more than 74,000 non-profit organizations around the country.
www.volunteermatch.org

ABOUT THE AUTHOR

On July 9, 1991, Peter VandenBosch, a private pilot and retired business-man, flew two children from Holland, Michigan—a brother and sister in need of specialized medical treatment—to the Mayo Clinic in Rochester, Minnesota. That was the beginning of Wings of Mercy, Inc. Twenty years later the organization he founded has flown more than 5,500 medical missions, started three chapters in two states, and recruited 300 volunteer pilots. VandenBosch lives in Zeeland, Michigan, with his wife, Joan.